PRAISE FOR PAUL FERRINI'S BOOKS

"The most important books I have read. I study them like a bible!"
Elisabeth Kübler-Ross, M.D., author of *On Death and Dying*.

"These words embody tolerance, universality, love and compassion—
hallmarks of all Great Teachings. They turn our attention inward to
our own divine nature, instead of diverting it outward. Paul Ferrini is
a modern-day Kahlil Gibran—poet, mystic, visionary, teller of truth."
Larry Dossey, M.D., author of *Healing Words: The Power of Prayer
and the Practice of Medicine*.

"Paul Ferrini leads us skillfully and courageously beyond shame,
blame and attachment to our wounds into the depths of self-forgive-
ness. His work is a must-read for all people who are ready to take
responsibility for their own healing." John Bradshaw, author of
Family Secrets.

"A breath of fresh air in an often musty and cluttered domain. With
sweetness, clarity, and simplicity we are directed to the truth within.
I read this book whenever my heart directs, which is often."
Pat Rodegast, author of *Emmanuel's Book I, II and III*.

"Paul Ferrini's writing is authentic, delightful and wise. It reconnects
the reader to the Spirit Within, to that place where even our deepest
wounds can be healed." Joan Borysenko, Ph.D., author of *Guilt is the
Teacher, Love is the Answer.*

"I feel that this work comes from a continuous friendship with the
deepest part of the Self. I trust its wisdom." Coleman Barks, poet and
translator.

"Paul Ferrini's wonderful books show a way to walk lightly with joy
on planet earth." Gerald Jampolsky, M.D., author of *Love is Letting
Go of Fear.*

Book Design by Paul Ferrini
and Lisa Carta

Library of Congress Number
2004110458

ISBN # 1-879159-61-9

Heartways Press
9 Phillips Street, Greenfield MA 01301
www.heartwayspress.com

Manufactured in the United States of America

THE POWER OF
LOVE

*Ten Spiritual Practices
that can Transform your Life*

PAUL FERRINI

Table of Contents

Introduction

*T*his book contains ten spiritual practices that can change your life. The practices are not difficult, but they do require a commitment.

During the first week, you will be asked to spend fifteen minutes a day doing a simple spiritual practice. Other practices will be added each week and your time commitment will increase somewhat as you go on. As you complete each practice, you will be ready for the next one.

It will take you a minimum of ten weeks to complete this program. So, before you begin, ask yourself if you are willing to make a commitment to daily spiritual practice for 10 weeks.

In my experience as a teacher, commitment is the greatest issue for students. Real commitment to spiritual practice means that we don't rush or try to skip over steps.

Most people are in a hurry to finish so that they can say they completed the workshop or the class. We ask you to bring a different consciousness to these practices. Bring your complete attention to what you are doing here. Be fully present and you will get the intended results.

The first spiritual practice is a foundation practice. All the other practices in this book build on it. That is why we ask you to give a minimum of fifteen fully present minutes to this practice every day for the first week. If you skip a day, or give less than fifteen minutes, regardless of the reason, please start over. When you have completed seven consecutive days of practice, then you may move on to the second spiritual practice.

Follow the same guidelines in subsequent weeks. If you miss a practice period during a given week start over with that week's spiritual practice. This is especially important with the second and third spiritual practices. Like the first practice, they are foundation practices.

Ideally, this experiential curriculum calls for 70 consecutive days of practice, but don't be discouraged if you miss a day here and there. Just start over for that week. That way you will be able to give each spiritual practice 7 consecutive days of practice. That means that you will have 70 days of heartfelt practice, even if it takes you 90 or 100 days to complete all the practices.

Our goal here is not speed, but depth of experience. So please be honest with yourself and give these practices the time and attention they deserve.

The program is very simple and does not involve an enormous amount of your time. The first five spiritual practices (in Part One) require only about 30-45 minutes per day of practice time. The next five spiritual practices (in Part Two) require an additional commitment of two hours per week and extend your spiritual practice into the community.

In week nine, you will be asked to set aside seven days for a spiritual retreat, so you may want to begin planning for this now.

Ideally, you would be able to attend one of our Spiritual Mastery retreats, but if this isn't possible you can design your own retreat following the guidelines in the ninth spiritual practice.

So let us review the agreements you are asked to make and the understandings you should have before embarking on this program of spiritual awakening.

1. You agree to be fully present in your practice every day.

2. If you miss a practice period during the week, you agree to start over on that week's practice.

3. You understand that this program is a ten-week program only if no days are skipped. If you skip days, it will take you longer to complete the program.

4. You understand that it is okay not to complete the program, and it is also okay to start over as many times as you want. However, you also understand that successful completion means 70 days of heartfelt practice.

Seventy days are a very small part of your life. Yet the 70 days you take to complete this program of spiritual practice may be the most important days you spend in your life.

The master Jesus spent 40 days and nights in the wilderness before he emerged and began teaching. Of course, he was an advanced student and he was practicing day and night.

I assure you that if you practice day and night your results will be extraordinary also. But we are not asking you for that.

Simply make the modest time investment described above and your life will be transformed. You will be significantly empowered as a human being and connected to the Source of Love in your heart of hearts.

To help you to anchor in these practices, you might find it helpful to keep a daily or weekly journal reflecting on your experiences. Make notes about any resistances or difficulties you have with each practice, as well as any successes or break-throughs you experience. Journaling is optional, unless you wish to seek certification to teach this material; in that event, it is required.

Please note that this book is intended to be Part Two of my *Course in Spiritual Mastery*. Part One is presented in the book and the CD series entitled *The Laws of Love*.

If you aren't sure whether or not you are ready to commit to the experiential exercises in this book, I urge you to work with the material in *The Laws of Love* first. It will provide you with the intellectual framework you need to understand and commit to these practices.

You can also do *The Laws of Love* and *The Power of Love* simultaneously. This will enable you to master one spiritual principle and one spiritual practice each week for the next ten weeks. This is an ideal way to experience this material.

The optimum time to begin this experiential program is at the new moon, or at least during the moon's first quarter. If the moon is waning when you read this, you might want to finish reading through this book and perhaps read the companion book *The Laws of Love* before starting spiritual practice #1. Or you can start right away and spend an extra week or two on the first practice, so that you move into spiritual practice #2 during the second quarter of the moon's cycle. This is just a suggestion. It is not a requirement, so please decide what works best for you.

If you want to explore the principles and practices in the first two books in greater depth, you can move onto volume three entitled *The Presence Of Love*. Our teacher certification program relies on this third book, along with the retreats and workshops that further develop the experiential aspects of the curriculum, to prepare people to teach this *Course* in their home communities.

I hope that you find this book to be a practical tool for opening up to the power of Love within your heart. And I hope that these spiritual practices will become a regular part of your life.

Namaste,

Paul Ferrini

PART ONE

Overview of Spiritual Practices in Part One

*T*he first spiritual practice asks you to commit to spending fifteen minutes per day in silence to connect with God, your Divine Essence. You are asked to perform this practice on a daily basis for the next ten weeks and to make it a regular part of your life. This is a foundational practice that will help you bring the presence of God into your life every day. All the other practices in the *Course* build on this one. That is why we ask you to start over if you miss even a single day of practice during the first week.

The second spiritual practice asks you to see and treat others as equals. When you judge others, it asks you to acknowledge those judgments and get in touch with the fear and sense of unworthiness behind them. This is a practice that you do on a daily basis whenever you notice that you are judging others. It is also a foundational practice that you will continue to do throughout the ten-week period as the need for it arises in your life. This practice will help you begin to hold your fears consciously and compassionately so that they no longer run your life at an unconscious level. This second practice will be a major step toward learning to love and accept yourself without conditions.

The third spiritual practice asks you to use the mirror of your intimate relationships with others to see the parts of yourself that you are scared of or ashamed to look at. It invites you to withdraw your projections from others and begin to face your shadow. It asks you to cultivate a relationship with the wounded child within and begin the process of healing your deepest emotional wounds. You are asked to continue this dialogue with your child in subsequent weeks whenever you are triggered by your partner or by other people in your life. The third practice also invites you to create a safe space in your relationship where you can own your thoughts, feelings and experiences, without trying to blame others for them. This practice will be a major step toward creating right relationship in your life.

The fourth spiritual practice asks you to take responsibility for creating what you need and want in your life. It asks you to be honest about what you care about most and can be fully committed to so that you can begin to harness your talents and desires. This practice asks you to formulate and enact an action plan involving daily, weekly and monthly activities. You will therefore continue these activities throughout the remaining six weeks of the *Course*. This practice will be a major step toward creating right livelihood in your life.

The fifth spiritual practice asks you to understand any patterns of self-betrayal that might be operating in your life. It asks you to stand up for yourself and make decisions that are best for you. It encourages you to get in touch with your core beliefs and values and to be honest with others about who you are. It asks you to be aware of the ways you may have limited yourself and boxed yourself into a lifestyle that aims to please others, and it invites you to step out of the box and risk being yourself. This practice will enable you to take a major step forward in becoming an authentic, empowered person who is capable of making conscious choices.

Spiritual Fruit

*T*he fruit is only as healthy as the tree and the tree only as healthy as the seed.

The master Jesus told us: "By their fruits shall ye know them." What are the fruits that he referred to? The fruits are our actions. Kindness is a fruit, but so is cruelty. Patience is a fruit, but so is impatience. Fairness is a fruit, but so is injustice.

There are good fruits and bad fruits. Kindness is a good fruit. Cruelty is a bad fruit. Good fruits taste good and nurture us. We delight in them and want to share them with others. Bad fruits taste bad and poison us. We want to spit them out.

Spiritual fruits are loving, empowering, compassionate. If we are on a spiritual path, these are the fruits we want to cultivate.

Generally speaking, a healthy tree produces good fruits and an unhealthy tree produces bad fruits.

If our fruits are our actions, what then is the tree? The tree is our character. It is our overall stance and disposition. It is our strength or lack of it.

Do we have integrity? Are we consistent and reliable, both mentally and emotionally, or do we constantly change our mind? Do we have girth, substance, deep roots in the ground? Do we stand up for ourselves? Do we shelter and protect others who need our help?

Some trees are strong and healthy. Others are weak and sickly. The former produce fruit that is tasty. The latter produce fruit that is unappetizing.

You may not be able to judge a book by its cover, but you can ascertain the health of a tree by tasting its fruit.

All actions that are hurtful to self or others come from a tree under stress. The fruit of such trees should be quarantined. One should not eat this fruit.

First, let the tree be rehabilitated. Let it be nursed back to health. Then its fruit can be eaten.

Today, most of our trees are weak and their fruit is damaged. Our lifestyles are ridiculously stressful. They do not and cannot support life physically, emotionally or mentally. Is it any wonder that people despair?

Yet despair is simply more dis-eased fruit. When sick people eat it, they get sicker.

So how do we rehabilitate the tree?

Remember, the tree is only as strong as its roots. Character is only as strong as the dominant patterns of thinking and feeling. Consciousness is the root of all action.

So if you want to address the quality of the fruit or the tree that grows it, you need to look at consciousness itself.

If you want to know how your life can be more harmonious, you need to start by looking at your thoughts and your feelings right now. What are you thinking? What judgments of yourself or others are moving through your mind? Are you justifying these judgments or beating yourself up for having them?

How do you feel right now? Do you feel loving and loveable, or are you feeling resentful and unworthy? Do you have anger and guilt right beneath the surface? Are you afraid and unable to face your fear?

What is your state of heart and mind right in this moment?

That is the root of the tree. That and that alone determines the strength of the tree, the quality of its fruit, and the ability of its seed to prosper.

Actions and their Fruit

The master also told us "As you sow, so shall you reap." What does this mean?

Like the fruit that falls to the ground and releases its seeds, our actions eventually take root in the ground and new trees grow from them. The quality of our actions determines the result that they bring. Just as good fruit yields good seed and healthy saplings, good actions yield good results and circumstances.

The whole intent of Jewish law from the Ten Commandments to the Talmud was simply to convey this simple understanding to us.

Jesus simply reminded us that we could not "fake it." We could not fool God or divine law. An unhappy heart will produce unhappy results, even if it pretends it is happy.

Whatever is within will manifest without. Consciousness gives birth to action and its results. The root of all manifestation is in consciousness.

That is why spiritual practice must begin here.

The Power of Oneness

The First Spiritual Practice

*T*here are two types of consciousness: Unity consciousness and duality consciousness. Unity consciousness blesses and includes. Duality consciousness judges and separates.

We experience unity consciousness when we remember our connection with God. That is always an experience of ecstasy.

We experience duality consciousness when we forget our connection with God. That is always an experience of suffering.

Unity consciousness can also be called Oneness or God consciousness. In order to experience this transcendent state, we must turn our attention from the external affairs of the world and look within to encounter God's essence within us. We do this by getting centered and breathing, usually with our eyes closed. We do not seek the Kingdom of Heaven outside, but within our heart of hearts.

When we take time to connect with God, we come into our center. We feel God's presence there. We may experience this as energy or warmth, or simply as a deep peacefulness. In these moments of connectedness, we feel loved, accepted and blessed. And we get in touch with our capacity to love ourselves and others unconditionally.

In many Eastern religions, daily meditation practice is considered essential. In many Western religions, daily prayer or reflection is encouraged. Taking time each day to enter the silence of our hearts and commune with God is perhaps the most important of all universal spiritual practices.

Practice 1

Communion With God

Today and every day this week, you are asked to spend at least 15 minutes going into the silence to commune with God. Many people find it easiest to set aside this time when they get up in the morning before they move into the demands and expectations of their work or family life. Others prefer to take this time at night before going to bed. Choose a time that works best for you and then let that time be your daily appointment with God.

Keeping the same time every day is important because it helps you build this practice into your life. You are creating a new foundation for living, so build it clearly and solidly. All other practices in this book build on this daily practice, so please do not move onto the other practices before you have integrated this one into your life for seven consecutive days.

Choose a beautiful spot in your home or in nature where you won't be interrupted. If you wish, build a simple little altar—a few stones gathered together—or a candle with some flowers or incense if you prefer. Create a space that feels holy to you.

Begin to do some deep breathing—inhaling and exhaling through your nose for a count of 5 or 7 or whatever feels relaxing to you. On the inhale let yourself remember "I am taking this time to center within my heart of hearts, to connect with the core of my being, where the Spirit of God resides" and on the exhale tell yourself "I am letting go of any worries or stressors that stand between me and my deepest peace. I am coming to God empty and open."

As you breathe and center, feel the warmth and peace of God in your physical body. Feel the warmth of unconditional love and acceptance in your heart center and the spaciousness and grace of God's openness in your mind. Let "Spirit" move within you, filling up every cell of your body and moving through your skin to surround you and anyone else whose life you share.

Dwell at peace in this moment. If judgments come, just acknowledge them gently, but know that you are not these judgments. Stay in the energy and the radiance. Commune with God as though you and God are the only ones there. Let yourself be in the consciousness of "I and the Father are One," as Jesus was.

As much as possible, remember your oneness with God throughout the day. Whenever you get drawn into the drama of life, step back and remember your connection. You and God are not separate because the Spirit of God lives in you and through you.

Extending Silent Communion Throughout the Day

As your daily practice takes root, you will find that you are able to re-experience this communion with God throughout the day. Sometimes, just closing your eyes and breathing deeply will enable you to reconnect to the energy of unconditional love and acceptance in your heart, removing you from the push-pull drama around you and restoring your inner peace and equilib-rium. The practice of "Remembering God" thus becomes an act of remembering the truth about yourself. You can quicken this process by taking five minutes out of every waking hour to close your eyes and re-enter the silence. This 5 minutes of God com-munion becomes your little mini-retreat from the world and sustains God's presence in your life throughout the day.

Stepping into Love Communion

If you have trouble connecting to God and your essential Self, experiment with the following process of "Stepping into Love Communion."

We enter into Unity consciousness by accepting life as it is right now. To help you enter this state of unconditional love and acceptance, allow yourself to sink into the awareness reflected in the following words:

> *I can accept myself as I am right now.*
> *I can accept others as they are right now.*
> *I can accept life as it is right now.*

These words are not affirmations to be mindlessly repeated. They are not magical formulas. They are statements of truth that represent a certain level of consciousness to which you can attune.

Saying these words if you don't believe them is an exercise in futility. So let yourself sink into the consciousness of the words before you attempt to say them. Breathe with the words. Mull them over. Turn them around and let them weave into your consciousness right now. When you feel willing to do what the words say, then they have meaning.

So be with them until that willingness comes. That is what it means to attune or to "vibrate with the words." Then continue:

I am loveable and can receive love right here and now.
Others are loveable and can receive my love right here and now.
Love can be fully present in my life right here and now.

Let this sink in. When it has, then continue:

I am the bringer of love.
Without my presence and my willingness to let love come
through me, love cannot be.
Without my presence, love cannot be.

Let this sink in. Breathe into this awareness. Love comes from you, not from someone else. Then continue:

I cannot bring love to myself or others if my heart is not open.
I am willing to breathe into my heart and feel it open right now.
I am willing to be open to the healing power of love.

Be in the consciousness of these words until the words dissolve and only their resonance remains in consciousness. Then you will experience the ecstasy of love communion.

You might find it helpful to write these words down and carry them with you in your wallet or pocketbook. That way you will be able to use them not just in your formal 15 minute meditation, but throughout the day when you are thrown off-center and need to come back into connection with the Source of Love within yourself.

Results of the First Spiritual Practice

This first spiritual practice helps to transform the following mental-emotional states that result from a sense of disconnection with God and our Spiritual Essence:

I feel lonely
I feel unworthy of love
Life is painful and has no purpose
I have no hope
I can't trust God or anyone else

Gradually, as we anchor in the practice, we feel a greater sense of connection to God and our own Spiritual Essence. As a result, our overall disposition begins to change. Our mental-emotional states increasingly reflect the awareness that:

God is with me
I have love inside me and I can connect with it
I don't always understand life, but I can accept it
Every moment is new and brings an opportunity
I am learning to trust

SUMMARY OF PRACTICE: *Take fifteen minutes to be in silent communion with God today and each day of this week. Extend this practice throughout the day as much as possible. Continue this core daily practice for the next 10 weeks.*

The Power of Equality

The Second Spiritual Practice

*J*esus gave us the key practice of equality when he told us "love your neighbor as you love yourself." The golden rule "Do unto others as you would have them do unto you" is another version of the same practice.

This sounds like a very simple practice, but you will see that it is more difficult than it seems.

Practice 2 A

See and Treat Others as Equals

During this second week of practice, let your intention toward others be to see them as equals and treat them as equals. Let the good of the other person be as important as your own good. Don't raise that person up onto a pedestal or try to put him or her down. Accept people as they are without favor or disfavor.

When you are successful in this practice, notice how it transforms the quality of your life. When we are in "right relationship" with others, there is peace in our hearts and peace in our world.

Right relationship means "equal relationship." It is a relationship between an equal brother or sister. It is the basis for mutual trust and mutual respect.

Martin Buber told us that when we perceive another person as an equal, we have an *I-Thou* relationship with him or her. It is sacred or holy relationship. It is an experience of heaven on earth.

By contrast, Buber told us that when we see another human being as anything other than equal (better or worse, less than or more than us), we have an *I-It* relationship with that person. That means we see him or her as an object to be manipulated for our convenience. We aren't concerned about the good of that person, unless his ideas, skills or resources are useful to us. If they are, we will treat that person kindly. If not, we will treat that person as an obstacle in our way.

Imagine, for example, that you are in line at the grocery store or that you are driving in traffic and you just want the person in front of you to hurry up and get out of your way. You are not connecting with that person in a human way. You aren't realizing that, like you, that person may be feeling impatient or frustrated. You just want him or her to move and so you begin to "nudge" him or her physically or mentally. Your behavior is "pushy."

Now what is a "pushy" person? He is a person who thinks he is more important than you. A pushy person isn't concerned about the well being or convenience of others. He or she is selfish.

A person who behaves like this establishes an *I-It* relationship with other people. This kind of behavior provokes irritation or resistance from others. It is the beginning of trespass.

Now, as Jesus told us, trespass begins in our minds. We can just be thinking "Hurry up, you jerk" and we are creating an *I-It* relationship. That type of relationship dehumanizes the other person and it also dehumanizes us.

Practice 2 B

Opening Your Heart to Others

This week, you are asked to pay attention to your stance toward others. Do you invite connection and equality with others or do you see and treat people as objects?

When you become aware that you are not seeing someone as an equal, just notice this and see if you can open your heart to that person. See if you can connect with that person as an equal brother or sister. Can you drop your selfish agenda and let yourself feel that person? Can you see that he or she is just as worthy as you?

This week you are asked to discover your equality with others on a moment to moment basis. That means that you are practicing with family members at home, with people at work, and with strangers in the supermarket or on the subway. Bring your awareness to all of your encounters with people.

Ask yourself "Is this *I-It* or *I-Thou?* Do I see this person as more worthy, less worthy, or equally worthy? Is my heart open or closed? Am I accepting or judging?"

Practice 2 C

Notice Your Judgments and Hold Them With Compassion

As you practice this week, notice the judgments that you make about others, and remember that a judgment can be a positive or a negative thought. You can look at a woman and think "she's beautiful" or "she's ugly." The first statement is a positive judgment; the second one is a negative judgment. But understand clearly that both are judgments. When I say "I like you" I am making a judgment; when I say "I don't like you" I am also making a judgment.

Your goal in this second part of the weekly practice is not to try to cultivate "good" judgments or get rid of "bad" ones. Your goal is simply to be aware of all judgments that you make.

As you feel more and more comfortable with this practice, go deeper with it. When you find yourself thinking "She's beautiful" ask yourself if you feel equal or unequal to her. Do you see her as "more beautiful" than you are, "less beautiful" than you are, or "just as beautiful" as you are? Do the same thing if you think "She's ugly." Is she more ugly, less ugly, or just as ugly?

Many of us think that our judgments are bad and we should make them go away. But I can tell you from experience that this strategy doesn't work. If you try to make your judgments go away, they will either intensify, or they will go underground.

When judgments "go underground" they drop out of our awareness. It doesn't mean that we have stopped judging. It just means that we are not aware of our judgments. So we walk around pretending that we don't have any judgments when we have millions of them. This is called denial.

No, I didn't say *The Nile*, because that is a wide river that you can't pretend not to see. I said denial, which is a river that runs underground. It's powerful, but you can't see it.

The goal of spiritual practice is to raise our awareness, not to lower it. We want to take denial and turn it into The Nile. We want our stream of judgments to be visible, not invisible.

There are many people pretending to be spiritual out there. They tell us that they don't have any judgments. They act "holier than thou" and think that they have the answers for us.

Well, they don't. They don't even have the answers for themselves.

You aren't going to be able to grow spiritually if you are unwilling to look at your judgments. You can't escape the confrontation with your shadow. It is a necessary step on any authentic spiritual path.

Many people try to skip over this step because they are afraid of it. They are drawn to teachers who promise them instant salvation. But in the end, they are disappointed. There is no salvation for any of us without coming face to face with our doubts and fears.

So take a deep breath and start looking at the contents of your consciousness. Don't be afraid to see all the ways that you feel "less than" or "more than" others. I assure you: you aren't the only one who is feeling like this.

Our goal here is not to stop you from having judgments — as many misguided teachers would ask of you—but simply to have you begin to be aware of the judgments that arise in your mind. Once you are aware of your judgments, you learn to hold them compassionately. You realize that everyone has judgments and they are not "bad, sick, or defective" because they judge. They aren't even "unspiritual." They are simply imperfect human beings with unconscious wounds.

Recognizing your judgments can be the key toward healing your wounds. It can show you where your real issues of self-worth lie.

Going Deeper

The more we observe our judgments, the more we begin to see how many layers of judgment there are in our consciousness. First we judge, then we judge our judgment. We beat ourselves up for being judgmental. But it doesn't stop there. The downward spiral of judgment continues: We judge our judgment of the judgment.

We have to catch this spiral somewhere. At some point we have to say: "Okay. I see I'm judging. It's okay. It's no big deal. We all do it." When we say that, we take the judgment off the judgment.

That is the turning point. That is the point when we bring love and acceptance. That is when we begin holding our judgments with compassion.

We begin to see that our judgments come and go, but we don't have to identify with them. We don't have to pretend that our judgments are accurate or that they can be justified.

Indeed, we can recognize clearly and firmly that our judgments are not accurate and therefore can never be justified. Every time we judge someone, we are perceiving something that is not true. All judgments and interpretations are subjective. They inevitably contain some distortion of the truth. We do not see what "is." We see what we want to see and what we are ready to see, and we ignore, hide, or edit out what we don't want to see or are not ready to see. In the words of Corinthians, we "see through a glass darkly, but not face to face."

When we judge someone, we are entering into an *I-It* relationship with that person. We are establishing the basis for trespass.

So we remind ourselves of that. We say "I know there is no truth in my judgment and I'm not going to try and justify it. I am not going to try to convince you or anyone else that my judgment is true or accurate. I know it isn't. I realize that my judgment is not accurate and it cannot be justified."

Seeing the Fear Behind the Judgment

If we stay with this process of observing our judgments, we begin to ask "What's behind this judgment?"

Before long, we realize that our judgment is not really about the other person, it is about us. So we take the other person off the hook. We say "I see this is not about you; it's about me."

If I make the judgment "she's ugly," I am not saying anything about her; I'm saying "I see her as ugly." For some reason I need to see her as ugly. Others may see her as beautiful or ugly, but this does not matter. What matters is what I see. What I see says something about me.

Do you know the statement "Beauty is in the eye of the beholder?" It could easily and correctly be amended to "Beauty and ugliness are in the eye of the beholder."

In other words, we see others according to how we perceive ourselves or, perhaps more accurately, "how we feel about ourselves."

The judgment "she's ugly" tells us right away that we don't feel worthy; we don't feel equal. We don't feel good about ourselves when we look at that person. But "feeling not good about ourselves" says nothing about the other person; it is our own emotional state. We probably aren't even aware that we are feeling this way.

But when we judge this person, we know that something is up with us. And when we own the judgment, we realize the issue is not that "she's ugly" but that "I'm ugly or unattractive." That judgment is the real judgment. It is a judgment I am making about myself.

So first I take her off the hook. I say "I know this isn't about you. It's about me. It's not that you are ugly, but that I think that "I am ugly."

However, owning the judgment and taking the other person off the hook is just the first part of the process. Once I know that this is about me, I need to take myself off the hook.

After all, the judgment "I'm ugly or I'm unattractive" isn't any more true than the judgment "she's ugly." All judgments are untrue and can't be justified. That's true about our judgments of others and about our judgments of self.

So that brings me a little closer to the truth. It's not true that "I'm ugly." What's true is that "I feel ugly" or "I'm afraid that others will think I'm ugly." There is a fear or a feeling of unworthiness that lurks behind my judgment.

So I take myself off the hook and bring some compassion to myself. I say "I see that I feel afraid or that I feel unworthy. What's behind all this judgment of others and of me is this fear that I'm not good enough and that I am going to be rejected."

Now I am coming closer to my wound. Behind my judgment is a wound that needs to be healed. Behind my pain and discomfort is a need for some love and acceptance. And I realize I need to give myself some love right now.

This brings the judgment trail to its end. It cancels my projection of my own feelings of unworthiness onto others. Instead,

I confront these feelings directly and bring love to the wounded part of myself.

That wounded part of me might be the five year old child who is hurt because Daddy paid more attention my sister than he did to me. You can usually trace these feelings of unworthiness back to their source and it is often helpful to identify where they came from so that they can be understood and released. That is the purpose of inner child healing work

For now, go through as many of the steps as you can, but don't rush or try to force your practice. If all you can do is become aware of your judgments without beating yourself up for having them, that is a genuine achievement. Stay with that portion of the practice for now and it will bear fruit.

The more skilled you become in the practice, the more you can tackle some of the advanced steps. Let's review these steps so that they will be clear to you.

Beginning Practice

1. Become aware of your judgments.
2. Don't beat yourself up for having judgments.

Intermediate Practice: *Take Others Off the Hook*

3. Realize that your judgment is not accurate and can't be justified.
4. Own the judgment. Understand that it's ultimately about you, not about the other person.

Advanced Practice: *Take Yourself off the Hook*

5. See that your judgment of you is not true either.
6. See the fear or feeling of unworthiness behind the judgment.
7. Hold your fear with love and compassion.

If you are able to go through this whole process, you will not only become aware of your judgments; you will also be able to release them. In the process, you will tune into some of your childhood wounds and begin to bring healing to yourself and integration to your psyche.

Most importantly, you will begin to learn how to hold your fears in a loving and compassionate way. This is a foundational spiritual practice. Some measure of skill with this practice is necessary to move on to the other spiritual practices in this book. So don't be afraid to take some extra time here with this practice if you need it.

Results of the Second Spiritual Practice

This second spiritual practice helps to transform the following mental-emotional states:

I am constantly judging other people
I am ashamed of this and afraid to admit my judgments
I buy into my judgments and seek to justify them
I am not in touch with the fear behind my judgments
I feel inferior or superior to others
I often treat others in an insensitive way
I don't connect with people at a heart level

The following mental-emotional states result:

I am becoming aware of my judgments

I don't beat myself up for judging; I know we all do it

I know that my judgments are not accurate and can't be
justified

I know that my judgments are about me, and I'm willing
to look at the fears/wounds behind them

I am learning to be aware of my feelings of inferiority or
superiority

I am learning to drop my ego agenda and be more sensi-
tive to others

I am learning to open my heart and let other people in

SUMMARY OF PRACTICE: *This week see and treat others as equals.
Notice when you feel "better than" or "less than" others. When you
judge others, be aware of your judgments and "own" them. Realize
that your judgments are not accurate and cannot be justified. See
that your judgments say more about you than they do about others.
See the fear that lurks behind your judgments and hold it compassionately. This is a foundation practice, so please continue working
with it as necessary during the next nine weeks.*

The Power of Reflection
The Third Spiritual Practice

The Spiritual Law of Reflection works in mysterious ways. It often bypasses our conscious mind and goes right into the deepest and darkest depths of our psyche. Its job is to show us what we have tried to hide from ourselves.

Our conflict with others is the energetic invitation to look within for the root of our discomfort. The pain that a relationship brings into our lives is meant to wake us up to the origin of conflict within our own consciousness.

Of course many of us are pretty dense and uncooperative and we develop a very high pain threshold. But everyone has a limit.

It isn't easy, but as we learn to look into the mirror that relationship holds up for us, we begin to realize that no one else can be responsible for our pain and discomfort. We must take responsibility for our own healing.

The mirror tells me that I love you exactly as I love myself: no more and no less. So if I am having trouble loving you, I can be sure I don't love the part of me that you are reflecting.

The most powerful question anyone in a relationship can ask is "How do I use my struggle with you to learn to love myself?" Unless both people in the relationship begin to ask this important question, they won't be able to heal their wounds or feel genuine compassion for each other.

Challenging Faulty Assumptions

Most people put the cart before the horse in their relationships. They assume that the relationship is about giving love to the other person and/or receiving love from him or her. That assumption ignores the fact that both people are wounded and neither one knows how to love or be loved.

So if you want to be grounded and realistic about your relationships with others, you need to change the basic assumption "I am here to love you and you are here to love me" to "I am here *to learn* to love you and you are here *to learn* to love me."

In other words, our relationship is not a love-in, but a learning laboratory. It's only a love-in in the romantic phase when we are drunk on ambrosia. But once romance fades, hormones stop raging, and reality asserts itself, the classroom begins to form. And then the question is "Are we willing to learn together?"

There are two things that are bound to happen in your relationship once you get comfortable enough to let your hair down and walk out of the bathroom with curlers or a mouthful of toothpaste.

1.   You are going to attack the other person.

2.   The other person is going to attack you.

If you want to survive the classroom experience, you have to be willing to learn from both of these eventualities. When you attack the other person, you have to find out why. How did you feel threatened? What fear came up for you? And when the other person attacks you, he or she has to ask the same questions.

Moreover, it won't just be your intimate partner who triggers you. One day it will be your son or daughter, your friend or your boss. Another day it will be a total stranger.

Practice 3 A

Look at Your Triggers

When you experience being attacked or triggered this week, make some time to go into the silence and ask yourself "Why does this person push my buttons? What don't I like about this person? What upsets me about his or her behavior? Does he or she remind me of someone from my childhood?

Does he or she remind me of a part of myself I don't like? What aspect of me don't I like or accept?"

Do the same thing when you find yourself attacking your spouse or snapping at someone at work. Don't just let these instances of trespass slide. Don't stuff them. Take the time to look at them. And record any insights that come to you in your journal.

Throughout the week be aware that anyone who triggers you is offering you a potentially important piece of information about yourself. Don't just blow that person off and reject the opportunity to learn and to grow. Be willing to hang in there and look at the parts of yourself you have trouble accepting.

Facing the Shadow

Each one of us has aspects of self that we like and those that we don't like.

The part of us we like and want others to see is called the Persona. The part of us we don't like and don't want others to see is called the Shadow.

We all lift our persona up onto a pedestal and drive our shadow underground, where it cannot be seen.

Unfortunately, this does not resolve the conflict between persona and shadow in our psyche but just displaces it. Instead of one world where both exist together, two separate worlds are created. Our persona lives in the seen or conscious world; our shadow lives in the unseen or unconscious world.

Our shadow hides behind our persona. We cannot see it, but it is there. And our persona is terrified that the shadow will leak through around the edges of its mask. Somewhere in the depths of our psyche is the belief that "If you saw me as I really am, there is no way you could love me."

In an attempt to avoid looking at the shadow, we project our anger and our pain onto others. We make enemies in our outer life.

Whether we realize it or not, our external enemies merely reflect back to us our inner enemy—the shadowy aspects we have locked away in the deepest and darkest areas of consciousness.

We can do battle with our enemies out there in the world or we can pay attention to the message they bring to us. The same is true for our intimate relationships. We can get mad at our partner for driving a backhoe into our emotional backyard or we can realize it was bound to happen one way or the other.

If we are brave, we will be willing to see and embrace the shadowy aspects of ourselves that are brought up by the relationship. We will learn to be more honest with ourselves and acknowledge our discomfort, our self-hatred, our fear and our anxiety. And we will gradually learn to hold our entire experience compassionately.

The highest awareness within the field of duality consciousness is "All aspects of me are worthy and acceptable." Shadow and persona, dark and light, high and low, strong and weak are all acceptable.

Triggers

To walk with our fear is a powerful spiritual event. For, whenever fear comes up, it draws the shadow with it, and thereby brings us into relationship with heretofore rejected aspects of ourselves.

When people trigger us, our primal fears rise up from the depths of the psyche and anger or rage may bubble up with them. Of course, we don't like feeling these intense emotions. We don't think that it's very spiritual. But, in fact, it is one necessary stage in the process of healing.

Every time we are triggered by someone else's behavior, a door opens connecting our conscious world with our unconscious world. If we are courageous enough, we will walk through that door and see what lies on the other side.

Practice 3 B

See the Triggers as Gifts

This week you are asked to bring a whole different attitude toward those people who trigger you. Instead of resenting them, attacking them back, withdrawing from them or running away from them, welcome them into your life as mirrors and spiritual messengers. Realize that they are giving you an opportunity to look at your own shadowy material. If they weren't there in your face, you wouldn't be looking in the mirror. You wouldn't be learning as much about the parts of you that need to be healed. So thank them for triggering you emotionally. Thank them for helping you to understand and get in touch with your childhood wounds.

These present-day attacks reopen the old wound. We could not look at the original wound when we were two or three years old, so we used some mechanism of denial to distance ourselves from it. But that wound has remained in our psyche and our energy field. It is running our life unconsciously.

Our intimate relationships are mirrors or reflective mechanisms that show us our childhood wounds. We automatically attract into our lives people with similar or matching wounds. Often, we fall in love with them and marry them or they are born as our children. Invariably, they trigger us at a deep emotional level, bringing up our deepest traumas so that we can see them and heal them.

If we can create an environment of mutual safety in our relationship where it is okay to look at our emotional wounds, then our relationship can be a vehicle for our mutual healing. Without that safety, however, mutual healing is unlikely. Instead, the trauma associated with our childhood wounds will run havoc in the relationship. We will project our fear and our pain onto the other person and the relationship will be destructive for both of us.

For some of us, this is the inevitable outcome of our intimate relationships. That is because we refuse to take responsibility for looking at any of our stuff.

Holding our Fear with Compassion

If we want to begin to own our stuff, we have to learn to acknowledge and be with our fear. We need to stop seeing our fear or our partner's fear as "bad." We need to stop feeling threatened by our fear and instead let it speak to us.

When we stop being afraid of our fear—running from it, trying to hide it, or attempting to give it to someone else—it ceases to have power over us. Instead of going underground where it gets its hooks deeply embedded in our emotional body, it walks with us.

Visible fear is less dangerous than the invisible kind. When our fear is conscious and present, it cannot take us by surprise and rattle our lives.

We might cry or shake or start breathing rapidly, but these are signs that we are letting our fear come up into our conscious awareness. By contrast, holding back our tears just buries the hurt where it becomes inaccessible. That means the hurt stays with us and we often forget that it is there, at least until it gets triggered and we act in strange and fearful ways that surprise us.

A person with an unintegrated shadow is a difficult and unpredictable person to be with, because he is two people, not one. Like Jeckyll and Hyde, he has two totally different personalities and one does not talk to the other.

One day he is helping old ladies cross the street and the next day he is molesting young children. For such a person there is an immense and almost unbridgeable chasm between the dark side and the light side of the psyche.

Yet the Jeckylls and Hydes of this world are merely extreme examples of the schism we all have in our psyches.

When we have the courage to invite our fear to walk with us, the chasm is crossed and the light of love reaches into the dark, fearful corners of our soul. There, in the dim light, heaven and earth commingle and the real human is born.

Contrary to the machismo images offered to us by Hollywood, the real human does not pull the trigger of an AK 47 while his heart hardly skips a beat. Rather, he is scared. He shakes and he trembles. Sometimes, in spite of his attempt to hold them back, tears come rolling down his cheek. Sometimes, when he is deeply hurt, he begins to sob.

His pain is our pain. It is the pain of the scared child within all of us.

Deny his pain and the shadow stays hidden. Acknowledge his pain and he emerges from the underground carrying his plate of heartache and tears.

We need to let him come to us. We need to put our arms around him and, in that longed-for and long-awaited embrace, be made whole again.

The Wounded Child Personifies our Fear

The wounded child is a metaphor for our identification with our fear and the shameful interpretations that go with it. Although interpretations vary in shading, they all result in the conclusion that "I am bad" or "I am unworthy of love."

By seeing this wounded aspect of ourselves as a "child," we learn to have compassion for this part of ourselves. We learn to see the child's self-loathing as a loving parent would see it, offering emotional support and correction for the untruths the child has accepted about himself.

Practice 3 C

Bring Love and Acceptance to your Wounded Child

This week when you are triggered, see if you can get in touch with the little kid inside you who is hurt, sad, or angry. Find the old wound that is being triggered and, instead of looking at the trigger, see and feel the wound.

See the little kid who is 2, or 3, or 6 years old. Feel how overwhelmed she is and how she has to lash out at others or shut down emotionally to deal with the cruel or insensitive actions of the adults or older siblings around her.

See that the child is terrified and speak gently to the child. Tell her "I know you are scared and it's okay to be scared. Don't worry. Everything will be okay. I'm here with you now. I'll sit with you, sweetie. Just lean up against me and let me put my arms around you . . . and when you're ready tell me what scared you."

By speaking to the child as a loving parent, you can reconnect with those wounded parts of your psyche from which you dissociated as a child in order to protect yourself from feeling overwhelming shame or pain. For years these wounds may have been forgotten or may have seemed inaccessible, but they don't stay hidden forever. Now, as an adult, you can create a safe place for old wounds and traumas to surface and be seen, felt and understood. As the child trusts you, her deeply buried secrets may emerge. Memories of physical or sexual abuse or some other trauma may come up for healing and integration.

If this happens, you might want to go through this process with the assistance of a trained therapist who can help you maintain a safe space for healing. You may also find it helpful to be involved in a support group with other survivors. Regardless of the number or intensity of your wounds, you need to take the time that is necessary to heal them. Re-parenting the wounded child takes courage and patience, but eventually the wounds are healed and the child is reclaimed.

It think that it's important to be clear that the wounded child I am referring to is not the adorable, well-behaved child you want to scoop up in your arms and embrace. He is sad, lonely, angry, and perhaps even hostile. He doesn't feel loved and often strikes out against others: yelling, kicking, screaming, hitting and calling names. He may even want to hurt himself.

The child's extreme behavior—from severe emotional withdrawal to unpredictable temper tantrums—is a reaction to the perceived rejection of others. To protect himself, he develops lots of emotional armor and a variety of aggressive or reclusive behavior patterns that push others away.

So don't think the act of re-parenting your wounded child is a pleasant or easy task. It means looking at the part of you that you don't like and getting that angry or withdrawn little kid to crawl up on your lap and receive your loving attention.

As you continue your spiritual practice this week, be present with that little kid inside you, especially when she is triggered. Be the good mommy or daddy who understands that behind the child's offensive behavior is a call for love and attention.

Notice how, as you give love, the child begins to calm down. She begins to relax and learns to receive the gift that of love and acceptance that you are offering.

It takes time and patience to re-parent the unruly little child of your psyche, but it does work. When the kid is loved, she becomes joyful and exuberant. She begins to dance and to play. A new energy is born within you and for the first time you feel genuinely connected to your own creative potential.

Creating a Safe Space with your Partner

If you are in an intimate relationship with someone, you are also in an intimate relationship with his or her wounded child. And it is inevitable that one little kid is going to be jealous of and competitive with the other.

Moreover, when one little kid has a temper tantrum, it is likely that the other little kid is going to go on the warpath or withdraw deep into the emotional tundra. So it becomes crucial that you find a way to create emotional safety for both little kids.

Practice 3 D

Creating a Safe Place for Both Little Kids

Before beginning your spiritual practice this week, make an agreement with your partner (or anyone else with whom you live) to set aside time as necessary to process emotional material whenever you or the other person gets triggered.

To help you own your experience—instead of trying to make your partner responsible for it—use the following boundary mantra: "Everything I think, feel, say or do belongs to me. I am responsible for all of it." Do not blame the other person for any thought or feeling you have, any words that come out of your mouth or any actions that you take.

Remember, if you are angry, the anger belongs to you. It does not matter why you are angry or at whom you are angry. We are not interested in the trigger here, but in the person who is being triggered. That's the one who needs to fess up and ask for help.

If you lose sight of this, you will project your anger. Instead of owning it and finding out why you got angry, you will try to blame your partner for your anger. This just obscures the real issue. Attempting to give artificial guilt to others only deepens your denial of your own wound.

So this week, when a conflict occurs with your partner or some other significant person in your life, don't attack or retaliate. Ask for a ten or fifteen minute break and take a walk. Breathe and get centered. Try to get in touch with why you got triggered. Own your pain, your anger, your hurt, whatever is there in your heart. Then, when you are ready, come back and sit down face to face with the other person. Agree that you want to have a space free of blame or attack. To facilitate that, each of you will have the opportunity to speak without being interrupted. While one person is speaking, the other person will listen and accept what is said. You are not listening to agree or disagree, but merely to hear and understand.

When you are speaking, make "I statements" not "you statements." Say "I am feeling anger" not "you made me angry." Don't make any assumptions about or attribute anything to the other person. Speak only about what is happening for you. Take responsibility for all of your experience and share it so that the other person knows what you are thinking and feeling.

Remember that you are not here to solve problems or come to agreement. You are here to listen and to be heard. Remember, the other person will not be able to hear you if you attack or try to blame him or her. So say what you have to say in a respectful and non-blaming way.

When both of you have been heard, agree to let everything sink in for a day or two before attempting to have any further discussions. Let your shared awareness work for a while. You may be surprised at how new insights come to both of you and the conflict begins to shift by itself.

Results of the Third Spiritual Practice

This third spiritual practice helps to transform the following mental-emotional states:

I am terrified by my shadow and avoid it at all costs
I am easily triggered by others

I have trouble acknowledging my fears
I blame other people for my problems and frustrations
I can't talk to my partner without making things worse
My wounded child is on the warpath or is emotionally
    withdrawn
Deep down, I feel that I am "bad" and unworthy of love

The following mental-emotional states result:

I am learning to look at the parts of myself that scare me
When I'm triggered, I own it and try to understand what
    triggered me
I am learning to admit my fears
I am learning to take responsibility for my happiness or
    lack of it
I'm learning to talk to my partner in a non-blaming way
I spend time with my wounded child when s/he needs it
I am learning that my essence is love and that this love
    can flow to all the wounded parts of me

SUMMARY OF PRACTICE: *This week pay attention when you attack others or feel attacked. Don't focus on the person triggering you. Focus on what in you got triggered and why. Make friends with the wounded child within who is scared and needs your love. Create a safe space with your partner (or with anyone else who triggers you) so that both of you can communicate how you feel in a non-blaming way. This is a foundation practice, so please continue working with it as necessary for the next eight weeks.*

The Power of Creating

The Fourth Spiritual Practice

*A*ll of us are creators. Our thoughts and feelings give rise to actions that create our reality.

We are creative beings. We cannot *not* create. The question is "Are we creating what we want and what we need?"

Actually there are two questions here, not just one. And you will need to answer both questions honestly before going any further with your practice this week.

Practice 4 A

Understanding What You Need

Take some time to go into the silence and ask "Am I creating what I need in my life? Do I have the resources I need to live with dignity and to support myself and my family? Is the rent paid, are there groceries in the cabinet and the refrigerator, does my son have the braces he needs?" You know the questions.

Your needs are different than your wants. You might want a Mercedes, but that is very different from needing money to fix your 15-year-old car or needing bus money to get to work. If you think you need a Mercedes or a Ferrari, you don't understand the differences between needs and wants.

If that's the case, you need to take the same crash course the Buddha took. You need to see what's on the other side of the gates of privilege. So put your credit cards and your checkbook in the drawer, leave about $20 in your wallet, take a change of clothes and your toothbrush and hit the trail. If you have enough courage, lock the door when you leave and throw away the key. See how you do trying to survive for a week without access to your trust fund. And please don't take your cell phone or your computer with you.

Needs are profoundly different from wants. Meeting your needs is necessary for your survival. There is nothing optional here. Your needs must be met. Your dignity and well being as a human being require that you support yourself and your family. In this sense, you might not "want" to go to work, but you might "need" to go to work to put bread on the table.

If you are an able-bodied person and you don't go to work to feed yourself and your family, you are not meeting your needs and you will not experience the dignity and self-confidence that come from this necessary human achievement. An important part of the concept of "right livelihood" is the willingness to work and do what needs to be done to support self, family and community. In this sense, an able-bodied woman or man on welfare is not engaged in "right livelihood."

That does not mean that some people don't need assistance to become self-supporting. A woman with young kids needs day care if she is going to go to work. A handicapped person may need special transportation or specially modified equipment. An unemployed person may need the government to give him community service work until he can find his own job.

Help and support are often necessary. And one should never be afraid to ask for a helping hand. But a helping hand does not give you a paycheck if you haven't earned one.

So be really honest with yourself. Are you taking responsibility for meeting your needs or are you expecting someone else to do so? This question has equal importance to the man or woman living on a trust fund and the man or woman living on public assistance.

Once you have determined what needs you and your family have that are not being met, please make a list of all the things that you and other family members can do to begin meeting these needs. Make a note of how and where you need help, if you believe help is necessary. Be sure that at least three actions on your list can be taken today or tomorrow, and that at least three actions can be taken in the next week.

Practice 4 B

Understanding What You Want

Now ask yourself the question "Am I creating what I want in my life?" What do I really want in my life that I have not fully manifested yet? Have I manifested my potential physically, emotionally, intellectually, spiritually?

What is the single most important positive change I would like to see in my life? On the physical level, it could be "get more exercise or lose weight." On the emotional level, it could be "get into counseling or a support group, find or improve a relationship." On the mental level, it could be "get more education or training, find a better job, or develop a creative talent." On the spiritual level, it could be "develop a daily spiritual practice or do service in the community."

Don't let me put words in your mouth. Develop your own list of what you want to create. Then rank the items on the list in the order of importance.

To help you prioritize, be sure to ask "What is most important to me right now, in the next month, in the next year?" This is a crucial question to ask because if you are not ready to create something in your life, you don't want to rank it at the top of your list. Place at the top those "wants" that you are ready to fulfill now and in the coming year.

Now choose the one or two items from the top of your list and ask yourself what you are doing right now to bring that desire or goal into manifestation. If you are not doing anything or if you don't think you are doing enough, ask yourself what you could be doing now, in the next week, and in the next month to create what you want in your life. If you need help to do any of this, make a note of the kind of help you think you need.

Caring and Commitment

The spiritual law of manifestation tells us that only what we really care about and commit to will manifest in our lives. For example, if you want to be a great pianist, you have to be willing to do more than sit at the piano once per week. You have to practice every day. If you are willing to practice only once per week, you don't care enough and you aren't committed enough to meet your goal. So you would have to revise your goal from "I want to be a great pianist" to "I want to play occasionally for enjoyment."

So now you are going to look at your highest priority needs and wants and ask yourself "Do I care about this enough and am I committed enough to this goal to do something every day to realize it?" And if the answer is "No," take it off the top of your list and replace it with something that you can bring this level of caring and commitment to.

Caring and commitment are important in addressing needs as well as wants. For example, if you are moderately hungry, you might not be willing to crawl through the garbage at McDonald's to find a half eaten hamburger. But if you haven't eaten in three days, you might be willing to do that. If you "need" to make more money, but you are still able to pay your bills with an occasional check from Mom or Dad, you aren't going to spend 20 hours per week looking for a job. But if you are unemployed and have no money in the bank, you might be willing to spend 40 or even 50 hours looking for a job.

That just tells you that some needs are more important or compelling than others. When you choose a need to work on, make sure it is a need that you are committed to meeting.

The same caring and commitment test should be used on your top want or desire. Ask yourself "How much do I want this? Am I willing to work every day to bring it into manifestation?"

Criteria for Determining the Degree of Your Caring and Commitment

Here is a simple way of determining how important a particular need or want is to you. Ask yourself: *Can I live without it?* If you can live without it, it probably isn't something you will be passionately committed to creating in your life. For example, if you ask "Can I live without food or water?" the answer is "No" and you will very likely be passionate in creating food and water in your life.

Now ask the next question: *Can I live with dignity without it?* In other words, "Can I feel good about myself if I don't meet this need or fulfill this want?"

For example, if you ask the first question "Can I live without getting a job?" the answer might be: "Yes. I could live on public assistance or on my trust fund." But if you ask the second question "Can I live with dignity without getting a job?" the answer might be "No. I wouldn't have respect for myself." In this case, getting a job might be pretty important.

The final question to ask is this: *Can I honor myself and give my gift to the world without meeting this need or fulfilling this desire?*

For example, if you ask the person who wants to play the piano once per week these three questions, she would probably answer "Yes" to all three of them. She can live with dignity without playing the piano because her real purpose in life is teaching math to little kids.

But if you ask the fourteen year old prodigy who started playing piano at age three and has just won a major international competition, she would surely answer "No" to the last two questions, or perhaps even "No" to all three.

So use these three questions as a yardstick to measure how much you care and how committed you are to your priority needs and desires.

Lights, Camera, Action

Well, surely you don't think that I had you make those two lists, prioritize them and choose your top need and want just to stash that list in your dresser drawer. There would be no point in that.

The fourth spiritual law is about manifestation, not about procrastination.

That means if you take the criteria test and you determine that the need and want you chose to address are important, then it's time to make a plan and put it into action.

Here's how to do that.

Practice 4 C

Making an Action Plan

Take a blank piece of paper and write the need or want you are going to address at the top of the page. Start with the word "Creating." So if you need to get a job, you would write "Creating a Job" and if you wanted to go to college you would write "Creating a College Experience."

Now please describe what you want or need to create in a paragraph of three or four sentences. So under "Creating a Job" you might write: "I want to work and I'm willing to do anything. I would be happiest doing something outside. And I would like to learn a skill." And under "Creating a College Experience" you might write: "I want to go to a college that has small classes and high standards. I want to study biology and I would like to compete in Track and Field events." Keep your description simple and practical.

Now make a list of all the things you need to do to meet this need or manifest this desire. Do this in a brainstorming fashion so that you list everything you can think of. Then underline those things on your list that you think are most important and choose three things that you can do today, three more things that you can do this week, and three additional things that you can do in the next month to begin to manifest the achievement of your goal. Your action plan might look something like this:

Creating a College Experience

What I can do Today:

Go to the library and get a book on colleges.
Talk to my biology teacher and my track coach.
Ask my parents what they would suggest.

What I can do in the Next Week:

Read the book on colleges and choose ten favorite schools.
Write to these schools and request a catalog.
Review the websites of these schools.

What I can do in the Next Month:

Narrow my choice down to five colleges.
Begin applying for admission to these schools.
Plan campus visits with my parents.

When you read this plan of action, you get the sense that it is practical and that the person who wrote it is highly motivated. Look at your plan of action from a similar perspective. "Is it do-able?" and "Does it show motivation?" In other words "Can you do it?" and "Will you do it?" Be honest with yourself. If you answered "No" to either or both of the above questions, go back and revise your plan.

Practice 4 D

Implementing Your Plan

You are now in the fourth week of your spiritual practice. If you began this experiential curriculum during the first quarter of the moon, this week's practice will fall sometime around the next new moon. It will thus be an ideal time to formulate and begin to implement your plan.

After getting your plan on paper, begin to carry it out by performing the three tasks you agreed to do on the first day and the three tasks you agreed to do during the first week.

Once you complete these tasks, you can move on to spiritual practice #5. But keep in mind that you will continue to implement your plan during the next six weeks.

Put your action plan up on the wall in a place where you will see it every day. Make a point of looking at it when you get up in the morning and when you go to bed at night. As you complete the tasks listed on the plan, check them off. If new tasks emerge that you didn't anticipate, add them to your daily, weekly or monthly schedules. Be sure not to overbook or overwhelm yourself. If necessary, cross off less important tasks and replace them with new ones that seem more important now.

At the end of the week, take five or ten minutes to record your progress in your journal and/or to update the plan that is posted on the wall. At the end of the month, set aside at least an hour to celebrate your progress and make a new plan for the next thirty days. That plan should also include daily, weekly, and monthly tasks. By then you should be well on your way manifesting what you really need or want. But if not, determine where you need help and ask for it.

No matter what happens, don't give up on yourself. If you have difficulty reaching your goal, try to understand why. Was the goal itself clear enough? Was it something you really care about? Was your commitment to reaching your goal strong and consistent? Did you undertake all of the daily, weekly and monthly tasks on your action plan? Did you have all the information you needed and, if not, do you have it now? Were your interactions with others positive and helpful? Did you respect people and treat them as equals?

Be honest with yourself so that you can learn from your experiences. Sometimes we have to fail in order to understand what impedes our eventual success. Perhaps we need to make changes in our goal, our commitment, or our attitude. Failure is not something to avoid. It is something to learn from. So try to acknowledge what didn't work and make a new plan that incorporates the lessons you have learned from experience. In time, you will see that these principles and practices really do work when you are committed to them. But the one important thing that you have to remember when you are attempting to create something in your life is that it doesn't always show up the way you think it is going to.

Dropping Unrealistic Expectations

Often we are successful in manifesting, but we don't recognize it because the result doesn't come in the package we were expecting. If we look superficially, we will not see the fruits of our labor. We might believe that we have failed when we have succeeded in a profound but subtle way. We might even think there is something wrong with us, that we didn't do it correctly.

Let's not be that foolish. A creator must not find his creation unacceptable or he will teach himself to fail. Let us see what we create with depth, with patience, and with humility. Perhaps what we have created is not a massive oak tree, but a tiny sapling just pushing up through the ground. If so, we must celebrate the sapling and care for it, watering it and tending to its needs so that it can grow. In time it will be the oak tree we imagined, but it will require patience from us. Caring and commitment are not just necessary at the beginning. They are necessary every step along the way.

Those who fail often shoot too high. They want to launch a rocket and are disappointed when a pair of sneakers shows up on their doorstep. They are looking up at the sky asking "where is my oak tree?" when the sapling is growing steadily at their feet.

The great creators set modest goals and work hard to achieve them. Thus, they make steady progress, build up their confidence in themselves, and win the respect of others. Because they take small steps forward, they can complete the thousand mile journey.

If you fail, do not beat yourself up. Find out why. Ask yourself "Was my goal unrealistic or inflated? Did I try to skip over necessary steps? Was I willing to do what was being asked of me or did I rely inappropriately on others to get the job done?"

If you ask all of these questions and you still do not understand why success has eluded you, there are only two possibilities. Either you are deceiving yourself, or the time has not come for you to reach the goal you have set.

If you sense the latter to be true, revise your plan to include stepping stones and focus on getting to the first one.

Surrendering the Destination

When we put one foot in front of the other, the journey takes care of itself. We don't always get to the destination we charted, but we get to where we are supposed to be.

Christopher Columbus set out for India and landed in America. He was not a failure, nor will you be one if life takes you in a different direction than the one you anticipated. Sometimes we know we have to board the ship, but we don't really know where it is going.

You see there's a little bit of the Divine Will involved in all of this. And sometimes it is stronger and more certain than our ego agenda. Once we get on the ship, the wind starts to blow and the destination is no longer up to us.

But that is not a bad thing. That just means it's time to let go of your plan and embrace God's plan for your life.

Of course, God's plan is your plan, just as it was Christopher's. He just didn't know it until he got off the ship.

One of the things that you realize when you get out on the open ocean of life with your oars and your sails is that progress depends not just on you, but on the size of the waves and the direction of the wind.

The process of creating—while it does have a common sense and a logical aspect—is often not a linear process. Sometimes you travel east and end up in the west.

Christopher didn't anticipate that. And there's a lot that you and I don't and can't anticipate. Fortunately, there's still a little bit of mystery in this, enough to keep us turning on our toes.

In the days of Muhammad, no one knew that there would be a bunch of his followers who would develop a strange but effective spiritual practice of turning around in circles. No one knew that spinning around would help the Sufi dancers find the center of gravity.

It's hard to believe that what seems to be stationary is actually moving at great speed. Yet that is what our planet is doing every day. Even now, while you are calmly drinking a cup of tea and reading these words the earth is spinning willy-nilly on its axis. Yet, in spite of that, not a single drop of tea flies out of the cup.

Yes, the process of manifestation is a logical and purposeful one, but it is also mysterious and unpredictable. Perhaps that is why our greatest creations are the ones that take everyone, including us, by surprise.

Results of the Fourth Spiritual Practice

This fourth spiritual practice helps to transform the following mental-emotional states:

I have important needs that are not being met

I have important unfulfilled desires

It's hard for me to commit and I don't know what to commit to

Supporting myself and my family is difficult

I am not living up to my abilities

I can't get focused in my life

I procrastinate a lot

I feel like a failure

The following mental-emotional states result:

I am meeting my most important need

I am fulfilling my most important desire

I am committed to a plan of action

I know I can create a way to support myself and family

I am beginning to manifest my talents and abilities

I am focused on what I most need and want to create

I am doing something each day to move toward my goal

If I fail, I will learn from my mistakes and try again

SUMMARY OF PRACTICE: *Identify the need and desire that you care about most and are most committed to meeting. Develop a practical action plan involving daily, weekly and monthly tasks. Implement your plan this week and in the weeks to come.*

The Power of Choice

The Fifth Spiritual Practice

*V*ictims are creators who are unwilling to take responsibility for what they are creating in their lives. They create a mess, think that they aren't responsible for it, and expect others to clean it up for them.

A victim feels powerless. Of course, he isn't really powerless. He could decide at any time to take responsibility and empower himself. But he pretends that he can't. And often people believe him. They accept his sob story. And after awhile he forgets that he is playing the role of victim and begins to believe that he really doesn't have any choice about his life.

This wouldn't be a problem if others just left him alone to engage in his delusional thinking. But generally, he attracts allies—other victims who reinforce each other's delusions—as well as saviors—those who need to save him from his plight, make decisions for him, or otherwise take false and inappropriate responsibility for his life.

Not only is the savior's promise seductive to the victim, but it gives him a person to blame if things don't work out. If the savior fails to deliver, then the victim's plight is the savior's fault. Needless to say, this blaming of others only further entrenches the victim in his role.

This is the story of all abusive and otherwise co-dependent

relationships. A victim inevitably attracts a victimizer or care-taker. One who refuses to accept responsibility attracts another who can't wait to take responsibility.

The problem is that caretakers and victimizers have a compulsive need to control others. Any responsibility they shoulder comes with serious strings attached.

Both victim and victimizer give up their power. Sometimes it is hard to see how the victimizer does that. But the compulsion to care for or control another human being stems from a deep insecurity and inability to take appropriate responsibility for self.

That is why victims and victimizers match. Both are refusing to take responsibility for themselves. Both are incapable of making choices alone. They are codependent. Each one needs the other in order to decide and each will invariably blame the other when the mess proliferates and becomes intolerable.

To be authentic, each must take back his power to decide for himself.

Free will is synonymous with our ability to choose. We can't be ourselves and give that power to anyone else; nor can we be ourselves and take that power away from another.

Each person must decide or choose for herself. That is an unwavering truth of our embodiment. Any attempt to interfere with another's choice is a trespass.

People who have a tendency to be victims or caretakers must learn to stand alone and make their own choices. To do that, they must often disentangle themselves from codependent relationships where boundaries are ignored and power and responsibility are inappropriately given to others.

What It Means to Stand Alone

Standing alone means that one values who one is and tries to live in harmony with his core beliefs. He knows how to nurture himself, how to set goals in life and how to move toward them. He finds appropriate work, supports himself financially, cultivates friendships, builds support systems, and learns how to live in a practical manner on planet Earth.

Standing alone means that one is no longer dependent on parents or other authority figures for support. She is not controlled by others physically, financially, emotionally, intellectually or spiritually. She decides where to live and how to live, what to believe, whom to be with, and so forth. She makes decisions for herself and takes responsibility for what she thinks, feels, says and does.

All this is part and parcel of growing up and becoming an adult. A true adult is not dependent on others or inappropriately influenced by them. She is independent and self-directed.

Of course, no one grows up totally before becoming involved intimately with others. Many people get married and even have children before they know who they are. Yet the less they know about themselves, the higher the likelihood that they will betray themselves or others in their relationships.

Taking time to know yourself is time well spent. It makes it easier for you to live in your own skin and be honest about who you are with others. That honesty and clarity make for less hurt and fewer aborted relationships.

This week's spiritual practice is about learning to empower ourselves to be who we are. It is about giving ourselves permission to be the unique, authentic person that we are. It is about connecting with our core self, discovering and valuing our talents, and making choices that help us to learn and grow into our fullness as human beings.

Being Authentic and Empowered in Your Relationships with Others

Mature relationships allow each person to be himself or herself. That does not mean that there are no moments of tension, trespass or confusion about boundaries. All relationships experience these moments. But, on the whole, people in healthy relationships appreciate each other as they are, without needing to fix or change each other. That means they are free to be themselves and do not have to wear a mask or adopt an uncomfortable role to be in the relationship.

The question "Can I be me and be with you?" must be asked about every relationship we have. Lovers and prospective partners should be asking it of each other. Children should be asking it of their parents.

If the answer to this question is "No," we need to know why. Is it because the other person won't allow us to be authentic or is it because we don't trust ourselves sufficiently to reveal ourselves completely? Or is it a combination of our lack of trust and their lack of acceptance?

Generally, the degree to which we trust ourselves and speak and act authentically will determine the degree to which we attract people who accept us as we are. The more committed we are to ourselves, the more we tend to attract others who like and respect us as we are.

Practice 5 A

Standing in Your Own Light

This week, please ask yourself the question "Can I be me and be with you?" in all of your interactions with others. Find out which relationships encourage self-betrayal and which ones encourage self-disclosure.

This practice is not intended to improve others. Its intention is to help you gain insight into your own maturity. So ask yourself "Am I holding back? Am I afraid to be myself fully with this person? If so, why? Do I feel this person would dislike me or reject me if I were more authentic and true to myself in the relationship? Am I afraid I would lose the relationship if I had the courage to be myself?"

Ask yourself "Am I making different choices than I normally would make to try to win this person's love and approval?" or "Am I letting this person make decisions for me?"

If you answer "Yes" to these questions, your spiritual practice this week is to reclaim your power and learn to decide for yourself. That may mean that you have to ask for more freedom, responsibility and respect in your relationship(s).

Do this in a gentle but firm manner. Say "I care about you, but I'm scared to be myself with you. So I hold myself back. I let you make choices I should be making myself. I don't want to do that anymore. I need to be free to be myself if my soul is going to flower in this relationship." Put it in your own words.

When you withhold part of yourself from a relationship, it creates an energy vacuum that is often filled by the needs and expectations of the other person. When you learn to show up more fully, that power vacuum is filled and the other person can see and feel you. Of course, that may create a new set of problems in the relationship, but self-betrayal won't be one of them.

If you are not a person who gives your power away to others, are you a person who takes care of others and makes decisions for them? Do you need to dominate or control the people who are close to you? If so, your spiritual practice this week is to back off and let others decide for themselves. That means you will have to give people more freedom, responsibility and respect than you are used to giving them.

It also means that you will have to say "No" when others ask you to play the role of caretaker, fixer, or problem solver. Tell them the truth. Say "You know, in the past I have taken this responsibility because I sensed you expected me to, and I wanted to win your love and approval, but now I think it would be good for you to do this for yourself. I want to empower you to make your own decisions."

Whether you take too much or too little responsibility in your relationship, you will need to work on creating a balance of power between you and others. Don't stand in the shadows of another or let another neurotically cling to you. Stand in your own light and honor the light of others.

To help you do that, work with the people you love to establish clear and mutually agreed-on boundaries that everyone is willing to respect. When those boundaries are crossed, speak up.

You can't be yourself when you are preoccupied with someone else's business, or when someone else is sticking her nose in yours. When you trespass on another, apologize, back off and give her the space to decide for herself. When another trespasses on you, stand up for yourself, ask her to honor her agreements, and be willing to decide for yourself.

This week, claim your freedom to be who you are and to make choices that are good for you. Grant others the same freedom.

Practice 5 B

Not Lying, Being Inauthentic or Hiding Behind a Mask

This week practice refraining from lying to yourself or to others. Tell the truth about who you are and let the pieces fall where they may. Do not edit yourself or twist yourself into a pretzel to please others or win their acceptance or approval.

Be honest about who you are. Come out of the closet. Tell your secrets to the people who need to know them.

Are you playing a role that you are no longer comfortable with? Are you unable to keep some agreement or commitment because your thoughts or feelings have shifted? Have you done something you feel guilty about?

We aren't asking you to flaunt the truth or to beat people up with it. That's the other extreme. But don't hide anything that is important. Reveal who you are, what you think, how you feel, what is important to you.

When you find that you are going to say or do something that is untrue or inauthentic, catch yourself and say "I don't want to lie about who I am. Lying builds walls of separation. I don't want to be separate from my true self or from the true self of others." Take a deep breath, let go of the lie, and have the courage to be who you are.

Practice 5 C

Limiting vs. Core Beliefs

During the week, make an inventory of your values and beliefs.

1. First list those beliefs—inherited from parents or other authority figures—that you have found to be dysfunctional and have discarded as impediments to your emotional, intellectual and spiritual growth. How has your rejection of these beliefs opened up new opportunities?

2. Then list those core values and beliefs that you have held all of your life and still affirm as important and true.

3. Finally, list those beliefs that you are now actively questioning and indicate why. How do they limit you?

Use your inventory to understand how spiritual growth and psychological change are a natural part of your life. See how you are continuing to outgrow limited beliefs and expand your consciousness to include new insights and awareness.

Practice 5 D

Breaking out of the Box

Sometimes we create a life around us that limits us and prevents us from being and acting in a way that is honest and true for ourselves. In other words, we box ourselves in. We create a prison around us.

Un-creating our prison often seems harder than creating it.

Getting out of the box seems much more difficult than stepping into it.

That is because in a strange way, we are attached to the walls that surround us. On some level, they make us feel safe. They are familiar to us. The idea of knocking those walls down seems pretty scary to us.

In truth, part of us wants to stay in prison and part of us wants to break free. Our challenge is to honor both parts of ourselves. We need to honor the voice that says "I hate this place" and the voice that says "It's too scary to leave."

Unless we understand how we are invested in living in the box, we can't possibly break free of it. So we have to ask "What's the payoff? What does the box give me that I am afraid to lose?"

The answer is usually some form of "security."

And we also have to ask "What's the price?" What do I have to sacrifice if I remain in the box?"

The answer is usually some form of "freedom."

Please spend some time this week thinking and journalling about these issues. Identify what your box is, what you're security payoff is for staying put, what fears you have about breaking free, and what freedom you would be sacrificing if you cannot break free. When you feel ready to do so, begin to share any insights you receive with your friends and loved ones.

The Ultimate Risk

Being ourselves is the ultimate risk. It is a risk that all of us—at one time or another—afraid to take.

We are afraid to let go of our security blanket. We are afraid

71

to let go of the past, even though we know that it keeps us in prison.

These fears stop us only when we think we must resist them. We don't have to do that. We can look at our fears. We can feel compassion for the scared six year old kid who is afraid to get on the bus and go to school for the first time.

It is not easy for the snake to shed one skin and grow another one. It is not easy for the caterpillar to go into the cocoon.

Change and transformation are scary.

But consider the alternative. What if our lives could not change? What if they were fixed? We would not learn from our mistakes. We would not have the option of leaving the box when our soul tells us it is time to do so.

"No change" is even more scary than "change," because it holds us hostage to our mistakes.

The great gift of free will is not only that we can choose the first time, as Adam and Eve did when they ate the apple, but that we can choose the second and third time.

When we create in error, we can recognize our error and learn from it. Our second or third choice can be a better and wiser one than our first.

Growth is possible. Consciousness can and does expand.

No matter what is happening in our lives at any given moment, we can choose something different. We are not locked in.

When we were given free will, we were given a golden key. We didn't know what that key was for until the door of our cell slammed shut. After beating our heads mercilessly on the bars of our cell, we finally realized that the key fit quite nicely into the lock and opened the door.

Every door we shut, we can reopen with that precious key. We can correct any error. We can forgive any trespass.

That is one powerful key. Jesus reminded us of that.

Have you made a wrong choice? Have you done something you regret?

What's done is done and you can't have that moment back. But you have this moment to make a new choice. Because of the gift of free will, each moment is the redeemer of the one that went before it.

This week ask yourself "What new choices do I need to make to redeem the old choices I feel guilty about?"

Results of the Fifth Spiritual Practice

This fifth spiritual practice helps to transform the following mental-emotional states:

I am a victim of circumstances; I have no choice
I am afraid to let others see who I really am
I play certain roles and wear certain masks to gain acceptance
I feel that I live in a prison from which I can't escape
I let others decide for me or I decide for others
I cannot forgive myself for making bad choices

Gradually, as we anchor in the practice, we learn to see how we give our power away to others and we learn to empower ourselves so that we can take responsibility for our lives. Even when we lack experience and confidence, we refuse to let others make decisions for us; even when others lack experience and confidence, we refuse to make decisions for them. We accept responsibility for our own lives and ask others to do the same.

This leads to the following mental-emotional realities:

I am a creator, not a victim
I am willing to reveal myself honestly to others
I am letting go of roles and masks that imprison me
I see the box I created around me and what its payoff is
I make my own choices and encourage others to make theirs
I learn from my mistakes and make new and better choices

SUMMARY OF PRACTICE: *This week decide for yourself, not for others, and don't allow others to decide for you. Drop your mask and be honest and authentic with others.*

Identify and affirm your core beliefs and question the limiting beliefs that box you in and keep you from being yourself fully. Expand your consciousness beyond the box. Claim your freedom to be yourself and give others the same freedom.

Review

Congratulations. You have now completed the first part of this experiential curriculum. You have made a remarkable start on your path of spiritual growth and integration.

This is a good time to take a pause and review any practice that requires additional attention. Sometimes, spending just a week on a spiritual practice is not adequate. As you probably know by now, you can easily spend an entire month on each one of these practices and it would be time well spent. So don't be afraid to slow down and take whatever time you need now before moving on to Part 2.

This is also a good time to reflect on whether or not your life structure is supporting your spiritual practice. The next chapter will help you establish a daily and weekly routine for living that will support your spiritual practice.

Often, it is necessary to make certain lifestyle adjustments before one can be successful in carrying out a committed spiritual practice. If this is the case for you, don't be discouraged.

This is not a race to the finish line. This is a journey of integration. It is progressive, but not in a linear fashion. Sometimes you have to take two steps backward to take one step forward. So please don't feel that you have failed if you take time now to work on lifestyle issues. You are simply being realistic and increasing your likelihood of ultimate success.

∼

The first five spiritual lessons and practices help us learn to be ourselves fully and take responsibility for our experiences. They primarily deal with personal growth and development.

The next five spiritual lessons and practices help us develop as social beings, putting the good of others equally with our own. They primarily deal with expanding our consciousness to include the well being of other people, our society and our planet.

Obviously, you cannot serve others if you have not learned to take care of yourself and if you have not begun to actualize your potential. In this sense, feeling confident with the practices in Part 1 is a prerequisite for undertaking the next five spiritual practices. However, no one else can be the judge of your level of mastery. Only you can decide if you are ready to move on.

Staying Grounded

In order to be successful in accomplishing the practices in this book, it is important to develop a lifestyle that supports our spiritual work. There are certain requirements for healthy living on the the physical, emotional and intellectual levels. So let us look at each one of these levels:

The Physical Level

Physical health and integration is best achieved by getting proper exercise, rest and nourishment. The physical body thrives when it has a routine. Eating, sleeping and exercising at the same time every day helps the body to regulate itself and builds a strong physical structure.

Cooperating with solar and lunar cycles also supports the body. That means rising early with the sun and going to bed at a reasonable time after sunset. It also means beginning projects at the new moon or at least in the moon's first quarter.

Spending time in nature on a daily basis is extremely important for health on all levels. If you can coordinate your exercise schedule with a walk on the beach or up a mountain path, you will recharge on many levels simultaneously. Also important are activities that connect one to the earth like working in the garden or doing other physical labor outdoors.

Healthy physical patterns are rhythmic and repetitive. They establish the ground floor of being on which you build the rest of your life. It is very difficult to find even fifteen minutes a day

THE POWER OF LOVE

to go into the silence if you are getting up late, rushing off to work in the morning and coming home exhausted at night.

Most people need to invest at least two or three hours per day in self-care. Self care means cooking for yourself, taking time to exercise each day, taking a bath or getting a massage when you need one. It means turning down stimulation and entertainment that interfere with getting a good night's sleep, and so forth. Most people know what it means for them. Yet few people are committed to caring for themselves. If you are one of these people, you would be wise to make this the first step on your spiritual journey. The next steps will be smoother and more satisfying to you once you have established a healthy physical routine.

The Emotional Level

Taking care of yourself emotionally means that you don't stuff your fears, your hurts or your anger. You pay attention to how you feel. You take the time to experience and integrate your emotions. You make the alone time necessary during the day to check in with yourself and ask "How am I doing? Am I loving myself right now? Am I being gentle with myself?"

Emotional health also means that we have time to give to our significant relationships with friends, lovers and family. We make time to communicate and clear up misunderstandings. When we are afraid, we hold our fears compassionately, instead of shutting our hearts down. We ask the people we love to be present for us when we need them and we show up for them when they need our attention.

We explore our fears and open to help and healing as we

become aware of the ways that we push love away or run away from intimacy. We learn to nurture the wounded child within us and others and we learn to be gentle with ourselves and others, practicing forgiveness on a daily basis.

We do the things that make us feel good on a regular basis. If taking a bath is healing for us, we do it frequently, perhaps every day. If picking flowers or walking in nature is healing for us, we do it every time we can.

We reach out to friends when we need emotional support and we cultivate our connection with a sangha or spiritual community where we can connect with others committed to similar spiritual practices. At least once per week, we gather with people to create a circle of healing that offers unconditional acceptance and love to everyone.

If you do not have spiritual community or support system in your life, you can use Spiritual Practice Number Six to begin to build connection and community in your life. Although many people try to walk the spiritual path alone, it is difficult to do so and not always necessary. Each one of us needs to belong to something greater than ourselves. We all need spiritual families where we can give and receive unconditional love and support.

The Intellectual Level

Mental health requires finding a balance between left and right brain activities. We all need a certain degree of intellectual stimulation which we can find from reading books and magazines, going to the theater or the movies, attending artistic or cultural events. We need friends and colleagues with whom we can discuss at depth the issues that are important to us. We need to learn new information and skills so that we do not get bored or complacent.

However, we also have to guard against information overload. Too much left brain activity can wear us out. This is especially true today when many of us spend hours per day behind computers. We need to know when we have had enough and turn off the computer or the television set and spend some time meditating in silence or walking in nature.

We also need to find a balance between using our brains for analytical thinking and using our intuitive capacities to express ourselves and create beauty around us. Too much thinking is not helpful. It disconnects us from our emotional and physical bodies. That is why disciplines like Yoga and Tai Chi are helpful. They reconnect our minds to our bodies and help us become emotionally present.

We need to build rituals and routines into our lives that give our brains a rest and help us connect thinking to feeling, reason to intuition, and mind to body. Breathing exercises like Pranayama and various meditation practices are very helpful in this regard and provide wonderful support for the related spiritual practices in this book.

Other Important Areas of Alignment

It is practically impossible to engage in the kind of serious spiritual practices contained in this book if one has major problems in the areas of one's work, health, finances or relationships. These areas need to be reasonably intact and stable if one is going to engage in a focused spiritual practice.

If you have lost your job or you are struggling at work, if you or a member of your family has a serious illness or other heath challenge, if you are in the midst of a financial or relationship crisis, you may find it difficult or impossible to do the practices in this book at this time.

Of course, you are welcome to try. But don't be hard on yourself if you find it is just too much for you. Take the time to address the area of your life that needs your time and attention now and come back to this book when your life has settled down.

In the mean time, don't be afraid to ask for help. Talk to an advisor, a counselor or a therapist. Join a support group. Connect with others who are experiencing similar challenges in their lives.

PART TWO

Overview of Spiritual Practices in Part Two

While the spiritual practices in Part One focus on self-development and personal healing, the Practices in Part Two focus on building the kind of spiritual community around us that will enable us to heal from our deepest individual and collective wounds. They are about shared healing.

The sixth spiritual practice asks you to bring compassion to your family and your community. It asks you to make a commitment to serve others in some concrete way and to be involved in a group in which you can give and receive unconditional love and acceptance. It helps you fulfill your needs for belonging by developing spiritual community in your life.

The seventh spiritual practice asks you to recognize your patterns of underachievement or overachievement and work through your perfectionism or feelings of failure so that you can develop your gift and give it to the world. It enables you to take a major step forward toward fulfilling your life purpose and achieving mastery.

The eighth spiritual practice asks you to understand where you need to heal and to connect with other people who have similar wounds. It asks you to extend a helping hand to those you can help and to ask for the support of those who can help you. This practice helps you realize that you do not heal alone; it asks you to identify your house of healing and to engage with your brothers and sisters there on a weekly basis.

The ninth spiritual practice asks you to go on a seven-day spiritual retreat to digest and integrate all that you have experienced during the first eight weeks of practice. Ideally, you would join us for one of our Spiritual Mastery retreats, but if that isn't possible, you are given guidelines for designing you own retreat. You might want to make arrangements to take time off and begin looking for an appropriate retreat center now so that you will be prepared when the ninth week of practice comes.

Finally, the tenth spiritual practice asks you to integrate into your daily life the insights and awareness you received during your retreat. You are asked to simplify your life and to detach from the drama of life so that you can begin to be "in the world, but not of the world."

The Power of Compassion

The Sixth Spiritual Practice

*F*ew of us grow up fully before life asks us to shoulder adult responsibilities. Many of us get married and have children before we know who we are or where we are going in life. Ready or not, we are thrust into the social matrix by biological forces we cannot resist.

The desire for offspring is built into our genes. We gravitate toward it without knowing how much the bearing and raising of children will change our lives. For most of us, parenting is a challenge, but it is also a bridge that connects us profoundly to other people. Caring for our children and interacting with other families usually becomes the centerpiece of our lives.

Families are the primary building blocks of society. They are the place where we learn to sublimate our individual needs and discover what is best for the group to which we belong. They are the context in which we learn the meaning of unconditional love and develop the ability to give it and receive it.

The Gift of Love

Many of us don't love others unless and until they love us. We respond to love with love. But we don't initiate love. We don't offer love to those who are disaffected or angry or mean.

Our love is conditional.

And then one day the newborn son or daughter looks into our eyes with total trust and adoration and we discover a whole new type of love that we did not know we had. It is unconditional love: the complete and unqualified love of one human being for another.

It is a mother's love or a father's love. It is both gentle and fierce. It says: "I love you now and for all time; even as you grow and change, you will always be my child, my dear one, the beloved of my heart." It is an unwavering spiritual love, the same love that God has for His children.

We did not know that we could love in that way, but most mothers and fathers find out that they can.

We find out that we can go beyond conditional love. When our child is angry or sad, we love him. If he is sick or hurt, we love him. If he does something stupid, we still love him.

And if we can love even one human being in this way, then we have within us the capacity to love all. That is what it means to be a father or a mother.

That is what it means to join the human family.

Jesus told us to love our neighbors. He told us that our love must extend even to our enemies. He told us: "Everyone in the human family—no matter how he or she presents in this moment—deserves to be loved without conditions."

If you can make a single child out of your body, you know that every child deserves your love. No, not just your child, but the child of your neighbor, and the child of your enemy. Every child deserves your love. And every child becomes an adult.

So whom can you ostracize or cast out of the circle of your

love? You may get scared or overwhelmed and try to make exceptions and justify conditions, but in your heart of hearts you know there can be none.

Every child is your child. If you have the strength and the courage to look into the eyes of any child on earth, you will know this as an unmistakable truth. Beneath all the disguises, behind the veils of culture and circumstance, there is one love. It lives in every heart. It shines in every pair of eyes.

Giving the Gift

Until we offer love without conditions, we cannot receive it. But as soon as we offer it, we can feel it. We can experience it.

"As we give, so do we receive." That is the great law of love.

Many people feel that love eludes them. They keep looking "to get love" from someone. But love is not something that someone else can give you. Love is something you already have.

When you express that love, it vibrates in you and all around you. It is like a bell being struck.

Others not only hear the bell, they feel it resonating in their heart centers, because that is where their own love resides. The same bell tolls for them that tolls for you.

You see, you can't really give love to someone else. When you express your love to someone, what you are really doing is awakening their awareness of love's presence within their own consciousness.

A loving person creates a veritable symphony of bells sounding in the hearts of other human beings.

Expressing your love awakens the love of others.

Compassion for Others

The Sixth Spiritual Law asks us to express our love and compassion for others. It asks us to become involved in helping others who need our support. It asks us to work for the highest good of our families and communities.

You may already be engaged in compassionate service to others. Perhaps you work as a big brother or sister or volunteer at a soup kitchen, a prison, or a nursing home. If that is the case, you are already engaged in some form of the sixth spiritual practice.

If not, please consider where you might be able to make a positive contribution to those in need in your community. Think about the gifts you have to share with others. Are you expressing these gifts adequately?

Meeting the needs of others brings joy into our lives and reinforces our self-worth. When we give to others who need and appreciate our gift, we get in touch with our spiritual purpose and begin to fulfill it.

Practice 6 A

Serving Your Family

This first spiritual practice asks you to bring unconditional love to your family members. If you are not giving your partner and/or your children the support and the attention they deserve, set aside several specific times during the week to do so. Don't withhold your love from your family. Don't be too busy to give them your time, attention and support. If you have a pattern of not showing up for the people you love, this is your opportunity to reverse that pattern. Choose something that you can do every day this week that will let your loved ones know in concrete terms that you are there for them. If possible, choose something that you can continue to do each day in the weeks to come.

If you do not live with a partner or other family member(s), you can do this practice with housemates or close friends. Otherwise, focus your energies on the next three practices.

Practice 6 B

Reconciling or Healing with Your Family

Whether or not we have people that we live with on a day-to-day basis, we often have unfinished business with family members we used to live with, either as parents, as children, or as siblings. If you have unhealed family wounds, this is a good time to look at them and to see if you are ready to begin to heal them.

Ask yourself: "Can I use the insights I have developed already in this course to approach these people in a new way, without blaming or shaming them or myself? Have I worked through some of my judgments and forgiven these family members and myself for the misunderstandings or abuses that happened in the past? Have I begun to bring love to my wounded child so that he or she can face the abuser or the one he or she abused? Is it important that I stop being a victim or a victimizer in my relationships? Am I ready to tell the truth with understanding and compassion?

If the answer is "Yes," take the next step in healing your

unfinished family business. Write the letter you have been wanting to write. Make the phone call you have been wanting to make. Don't be afraid to stand up and reach out. However, be prepared for the possibility that, although you may be ready to heal, the other person(s) may not be ready. If that is the case, don't beat yourself up. Don't condemn the other person. Just acknowledge that "it is not time" for a reconciliation.

Even if the other person does not respond the way you want him or her to, it doesn't mean that your overture has had no impact. It may take time for others to work through their own pain and open up to the possibility of healing. Even if the door of the heart opens just a crack, this is significant.

Accept what happens and know that you can continue to heal, even if others are not ready to heal with you. The more you heal, the more deeply you will be able to hold the space for others.

If it seems appropriate, gather together with other people who have similar family wounds when you start or join your support group (see Practice 6 D below). These people then become your spiritual family, holding the space for you to heal when your family of origin is unwilling to join you or support you.

Practice 6 C

Serving Your Community

During the week, reach out to someone in your community who needs support or help. You can do this formally by volunteering to help on a weekly basis at some non-profit service organization in your community.

Or you can do it informally and spontaneously through random or not-so-random acts of kindness. If you see someone struggling to carry groceries, volunteer to help. If someone needs a ride or a place to stay, raise your hand and offer it. Whenever life presents you with an opportunity to be a Good Samaritan, seize that opportunity. At least once each day go out of your way to help others. Perhaps in the past you would have said "No" or looked the other way, but this week say "Yes" and do not turn away from a brother or sister who needs help.

As you practice serving others, notice when you get stuck, when you feel selfish or greedy, when you don't want to share your time or your resources with others. If possible, open your mind and heart at such times. Offer to share when normally you would not. Be generous with your praise, your money, your encouragement when you would normally be tightlipped and tightfisted. Appreciate others when you would normally be critical of them or competitive with them.

Practice 6 D

Starting or Joining a Support Group

This practice asks you to take a concrete step toward building spiritual community in your life. Please refer to my book *Living in the Heart: The Affinity Process and the Practice of Unconditional Love and Acceptance* for guidelines on how to create a loving and supportive group where people are accepted as they are and listened to deeply.

Let other people know what you are doing and invite them to join your group. Don't just ask your friends. Be brave and reach out to others you don't know. Find a group of folks who are not being served in your community. Even better, make contact with people who share your family-of-origin wound. Then use the guidelines in *Living in the Heart* to offer *The Affinity Process* to that group of people.

Not sure where to begin? What about the high school your teenager attends, the YMCA, a Girl's Club, a hospital, a prison, a nursing home, or a shelter for battered women? There is no scarcity of places where people need to learn to connect with love.

If you have trouble assembling a group of people, find at least one person to be your *Affinity Friend* and meet once per week for the next five weeks, following the guidelines in *Living in the Heart*. You will be on your way toward creating spiritual community in your life.

The Hands of God

As you carry out your spiritual practices this week, ask God to bring into your life people who need the gifts you have to offer and be willing to give these gifts when someone asks for them, even if it doesn't happen in the way you expect. Give freely without any expectation of return.

At the same time, if there is a gift you need to receive, ask God to bring into your life people who can offer you that gift, and be prepared to receive it, even if it doesn't come in the way or in the form you expect it to.

Each one of us is one of the Hands of God. It is through us that the gifts of God are given.

Agape love comes from one brother or sister to another.

There is no more powerful expression of our humanity than to be a channel or a vehicle through which the love of God flows.

Since God knows what your brother or sister needs, you do not need to know. You do not have to have a plan for loving others. Just be willing to express your love and the plan will unfold.

The willingness to serve and to be of use is all that is necessary. Spiritual gifts cannot be given or received without this willingness from both the giver and the receiver.

Remember, the gift does not come from you. It comes through you. The gift comes from God. So you cannot take credit for it.

If you need credit or a reward for giving, you are giving with strings attached. That means that you are attempting to give through your ego. And that never works.

To serve is to give freely without expectation of return. That is why service to others is a spiritual act.

Don't be ashamed if your ego gets involved. It happens to all of us. Just recognize that your need for credit pulls the energy back toward you so that it cannot extend toward others.

Cultivating Compassion

Compassion for others comes from our appreciation of our common pain, hurt, struggle, and suffering as human beings. Regardless of our race or cultural background, our gender or sexual orientation, our religion, our social or economic status, we all suffer when we get sick or injured or a loved one dies. We sympathize with the pain of others because we know what it is like to have that pain.

Compassion in war is rare, because there is an attempt to

demonize our enemies and see them as less than human. When we look at any group of people and think that its pain and suffering is not as significant as our own, we withhold compassion.

Compassion is a natural expression of our perception of equality. That expression is aborted when we insist erroneously that some people are not equal to others.

Withholding compassion is unnatural. To withhold compassion from any brother or sister, we must de-humanize him or her. We must believe that he or she is less worthy than we are.

We all want to believe that we are compassionate. But every one of us, if we are honest, has moments when we perceive others as less than equal to us and withhold our love and compassion from those people.

So, as you endeavor to serve others this week, be aware of the times when you find yourself withholding your compassion from others. When you do not feel sympathy for another person's suffering, ask yourself "Why?" What judgments are you carrying toward that person or that group of people? Can you see how your judgments of this person or this group of people disturb your peace and make you feel less secure?

Jesus told us "judge not lest you be judged." When we question the worthiness of another person or group, we invite them to question our worth as well. The result is that both sides feel less safe and secure.

Which do we prefer: mutual respect or mutual condemnation? We might have to work harder to achieve mutual respect, but it adds significantly to the quality of our lives.

Mutual condemnation means that both people lose. Mutual respect means that both people win.

Anyone, no matter how accepting and compassionate, can benefit from this practice. For all of us there are many subtle ways in which we withhold compassion from others and refuse to acknowledge our equality with them.

Bringing our awareness here is powerful. Every time we realize that we are not offering compassion, we find a way to connect with the compassionate presence within. Our awareness that we are not loving opens the connection to love.

We don't have to make love happen. It happens naturally and spontaneously. When we realize that we are standing in the way, we can move aside and allow the power of love to manifest fully in our lives.

Results of the Sixth Spiritual Practice

This week's practice helps us recognize and transform the experience of:

Selfishness (putting our own needs before those of others)
Feeling isolated, lonely, ostracized or cut off from others
Giving conditionally (with expectations of reward or credit)
Holding back our gift and denying our capacity to serve
Withholding our compassion (being insensitive to or in denial of the pain of others)

It helps us to cultivate the experience of:

Generosity (putting the needs of others first)
Feeling connected to others and part of a community
Giving without strings attached

Understanding why our gift matters and not being afraid to
offer it

Feeling sympathy for the pain and suffering of others

SUMMARY OF PRACTICE: *Make time this week to be compassionate and supportive toward your family and closest friends. Begin to
address family of origin wounds by seeking to forgive and reconcile
with estranged family members. Offer your time in service to others in your community who need your help. Start or join a weekly
support group that will enable you to give and receive unconditional love.*

The Power of Perfection

The Seventh Spiritual Practice

One of the frustrating aspects of embodied life is that perfection is impossible, yet everyone wants to be perfect. Often, in our quest for perfection, we crucify ourselves or others.

When we insist on perfection for ourselves, we block the free expression of our creative energy. This energy expresses best when we are able to drop our expectations of the outcome. Then we can experiment. We can play. We can trust.

Without trust in ourselves and our creative process, very little can get expressed. Insisting that our expression be "perfect" puts a lot of pressure on us and inhibits the spontaneous flow of our energy. We are afraid to express ourselves because others might criticize us or reject us. Or we are so critical of our own creative effort that we feel discouraged and reluctant to try again.

It is true that most of us are our worst critics. Anything that anyone else can say about our work, we have probably thought of and said to ourselves hundreds of times. Yet it is always difficult to hear criticism from others. We can't help but take feedback personally—even if it is offered in a professional way.

We want people to like us. We also want people to like what we create. Often, it's hard to understand that someone could like us and not be thrilled by something we have created. "If you don't like my art, then you don't like me," we conclude.

Perfecting, not Perfection

The irony of the seventh spiritual law is that while there is no perfection per se, the process of perfecting or making our creations better and better is an important one. That is how we achieve mastery.

Intense practice is necessary to master any skill. And practice of course means making lots of mistakes. If we are not willing to forgive our mistakes, if we are not willing to be gentle with ourselves at the same time that we strive to do better, our practice will be counterproductive.

Commitment to our creative process requires two equally important and seemingly contradictory assumptions:

1. Whatever we do is good enough.
2. We can still make it better.

If we make the first assumption, but not the second one, we are unlikely to improve our skills. If we make the second assumption, but not the first, we will be so hard on ourselves that creating will cease to be a joyful act.

We need to make both assumptions.

Both humility and self-confidence are necessary for a healthy creative process in which one refines one's skills and learns from one's mistakes. A little self-criticism can be helpful; a lot is not.

Sometimes, it is helpful to split the creative process into two sequential stages. Stage one is about trust and expression. We brainstorm. We suspend our critical faculties and just let our energy express spontaneously.

Stage two is about reviewing, revising, tweaking, editing,

refining. It is about giving a more precise form to the content we have expressed.

For many people who have a strong analytical side, this division of the process is necessary. It gives them permission to let go, trust, and express, knowing that they will come back, scrutinize, and improve their creation later.

For others whose left and right brain functions are more integrated, both trust and scrutiny may happen simultaneously. Yet either way, both the associative and analytical functions must be there. Content and form must integrate.

All life is creative and each one of us is a creator. So these issues are not relevant only to painters and musicians. They are just as relevant to electricians and carpenters.

Each one of us has a left brain and a right brain. For some of us, one side might be stronger than the other, but we all have to honor both aspects of ourselves. We all have to find ways to integrate and find balance within our consciousness and experience.

Sometimes it is helpful to look at the extremes to see how balance and integration can occur for us.

Meeting the Critic and the Fan

One extreme is the Critic. The Critic is concerned with form and practicality. The Critic wants relevance. He wants marketability, good reviews or professional acclaim. He wants demonstrable success. The Critic needs to be able to measure his creation favorably against other creations. For the Critic, only a few creative works are really "good." Most are average or just not worth bothering about. The Critic would never praise a symphony that was badly played, even if the musicians were inspired.

The other extreme is the Fan. The Fan can be your mother, your spouse, or your best friend. To this person, everything you do is great. It doesn't matter if you played some wrong notes. The Fan tells you, "Forget about it. It's not important. The orchestra played with inspiration and you were magnificent." The Fan appreciates the effort you put into it. S/he is focused on the process more than on the result.

If you grow up with the Critic as Mom or Dad you are always trying to please. You feel that your self-worth is dependent on how well you perform. No matter how much you practice or how beautifully you perform, you know the Critic will say it could have been better. So you continue to strive for a mistake-free performance, hoping that it will win Mom's or Dad's love and approval.

Since there are no mistake-free performances—or at least no performances that can't be made better—you are doomed from the start. That's the downside of growing up with the Critic. There is no way that you can win. As you might expect, that doesn't do much for your self-esteem.

The plus side of growing up with the Critic is that you work very hard to gain acceptance and approval. You become an achiever or an overachiever. And, if you have talent, you begin to master your art or craft. It doesn't matter if your art happens with a brush or a keyboard or if it happens with a basketball or a tennis racket. The themes are the same.

By contrast, if you grow up with the Fan as Mom or Dad, you are going to get lots of praise and acceptance just for being who you are. That's very helpful emotionally. You know that you are okay and that people love you. But little may be expected of you and you may not develop your abilities because you don't have to work to win anyone's approval. So you may become a couch potato or an underachiever. You may never develop the discipline and emotional toughness you need to succeed on your own.

Ideally, we would have both the Critic and the Fan in our locker room or on our bench. That way we could have balance and perspective in our lives. We could master our craft and still know that mistakes are acceptable.

But most of us don't have that kind of synergy on the bench, in the home or in the boardroom. Even if both the Critic and the Fan are present in our lives, the voice of one of these is usually stronger and tends to shape our psychological profile.

Practice 7 A

Determine Whether The Critic or the Fan is Your Dominant Influence

This week you are asked to determine which one of these voices—the voice of the Critic or the voice of the Fan—is strongest for you. Are you an underachiever and a procrastinator who lacks drive and discipline? Or are you an overachiever who is always taking on responsibility and jumping through endless hoops looking for applause?

Is your creative energy repressed because you lack confidence in yourself or feel that your gift won't be good enough? Or are you expressing your creative energy compulsively, because you need the approval of others?

Either of these extremes tends to be problematic. If you are an chronic underachiever, afraid to take a risk or step up to a challenge because you might fail and be humiliated, you will not realize your talents or learn to express your gift. If, on the other hand, you are a chronic overachiever who insists on jumping through hundreds of hoops to please or pacify others, your gift won't be appreciated or valued, and you won't get the love and acceptance you crave.

All of us have dysfunctional patterns here. We need to understand these patterns if we are to break free of them.

The underachiever needs to risk achieving something worthwhile or she will always feel "unworthy" and "less than others." For her, hard work and discipline are important and so are the rewards that result from making a commitment.

The overachiever needs to know that he can be loved and accepted for who he is, even if he puts down his violin or his tennis racket. He doesn't have to be Superman any more. He can just be Clark, one of the guys or gals.

The underachiever needs our support in stepping up to the plate. The overachiever needs our support in sitting down and letting someone else get up there.

Which one are you? Or what combination of both are you?

If you are an overachiever, you need to focus on developing existential self worth. Your spiritual work will be found in the corresponding section of text below. If you are an underachiever, you need to focus on moving through your fear of failure. That particular piece of work is described in the second section below.

Developing Existential Self Worth

A Spiritual Practice for the Overachiever

Self-Improvement books have proliferated dramatically over the last fifty years. It seems that everyone wants to improve something. Some people are looking to improve the way they look. They buy books on losing weight or exercising or taking care of their skin. Others want to improve their communication skills, their sex lives, or the quality of their relationships.

With so much energy invested in wanting to be better than we think we are, we forget one important thing: We are already okay the way we are.

If you don't know that, you have never met the Fan. And if you haven't met him or her, you certainly won't have internalized that voice in your psyche. So this is where your work lies.

You need to know that there is something that you can never improve because it is not improvable and there is something that you can never fix because it can't be broken. Do you know what that is?

It is your essential Self or your Spiritual Essence. It is the spark of divinity within you.

When you rest in this center of your being, there is absolute and unconditional perfection. When you rest in this place, you know that you are okay, others are okay, and everything that happens is unfolding as it needs to.

Another way of putting this is: You know that deep down underneath all of the events and circumstances in your life, God is in charge. And, if God is in charge, then all is well. This is the recognition of the *spiritual perfection* of life. Things may appear to be imperfect on the surface, but beneath it, spiritual purpose or law can be found at work.

Knowing this, there is no need to strive to be better than you are. You can never be more worthy of love than you are right now. There will never be a time or a place when God will love and accept you more than right here and right now. And that is true for any moment. You just need to tune into this.

When we are in this place, we can throw all the self-improvement books away. We don't need to lose weight or clear up our zits or improve our erections to win God's love. God does not love us less if we are fat, pimply or impotent.

The question is "Do we love ourselves less?" And if the answer is "Yes," then we will be addicted to self-improvement books and we will spend most of our lives in the futile pursuit of trying to be better than we are.

This is the false search for perfection. It is the search for worldly perfection, which does not exist. We needn't be ashamed of it, because we are all doing it.

It doesn't matter if we are seeking a perfect body or a perfect relationship; perfection in this sense is an illusion. Even if you manage to convince yourself that you have achieved perfection in these areas, you will still be haunted by the fear that there is someone else who has a better body or a better relationship than you do. And that fear will be the cross that you carry.

Every cross is made with heavy wood. After you carry it for a while you get exhausted. So why not put the cross down? Your job is to end this futile search and get in touch with your essential worth and goodness. That was a gift that was given to you before you came into this embodiment and you will be lost here if you don't remember this gift. Indeed, your spiritual health depends on it.

Your spiritual practice is a simple one: *know that you are okay, others are okay, and the universe is okay, just the way you are right here and right now.* Recognize the inherent spiritual perfection of life as it is. When you start finding fault with yourself or others, or when you think something needs to be improved or fixed, remember these words and let them sink into the core of your being.

Be specific. If you have the thought "I need to make more money" tell yourself "It's okay for me to make more money, but doing so won't make me better or more worthy than I am right now. My worth is not dependent on how much money I make." Let that truth sink in.

Moving through the Fear of Failure:

A Spiritual Practice for the Underachiever

Now, if you fall on a different end of the spectrum, your practice will be a bit different. If you are well acquainted with the Fan and have no trouble internalizing him or her, then your practice must focus on your relationship with the Critic.

You may have spent your life avoiding a confrontation with this character. But sooner or later, you won't be able to cross to the other side of the street when the Critic appears. Life inevitably brings you face to face with everything you try to avoid.

You cannot work though your fears as long as you try to avoid dealing with them. Only when you acknowledge your fears can you begin to walk through them.

So say hello to the Critic. Be honest and tell him or her: "You know, I am absolutely terrified of you. That's why I don't trust myself and don't express my creative energies. I'm so afraid that I am going to do it wrong. Or, maybe I know I can do it well enough, but I'm afraid that you will find fault with what I do and I will be devastated and I will never want to try again." Tell the truth, whatever the truth is.

And then tell the Critic "I have a hard time not taking any kind of criticism personally, so please try to be gentle with me. If you have some suggestions to make, please make them in a loving and supportive way. Otherwise, I might not be able to hear them."

If you are anorexic and feel that you are "fat" it doesn't matter that you weigh only 90 pounds. You are going to approach the scale as if you weighed 350 pounds. If you can't take criticism, you are going to freak out if someone just looks at you a little funny. You aren't going to take into consideration that her boyfriend just yelled at her or that she just inhaled too deeply when she did her nails.

When you are fearful, you don't have any perspective. So you just have to own the fear and ask people to be gentle with you.

Your spiritual practice is also a simple one: *Come out of your hole in the ground and be seen and heard. Express yourself. Don't let your fear hold you back. Tell people it's scary for you, but start walking through your fear.*

Believe in yourself and don't worry if you make a mistake. Just know that you will get through this and everything will be all right. Take a risk, even if you think you are making a fool of yourself. Your issue is trust: trusting yourself, trusting others, trusting life itself.

When you have learned to trust a little and have gained some confidence, you will realize that you are more resilient than you think. You can take a little criticism without shriveling up or running away. You can admit your mistakes and learn from them. You can be gentle and forgiving with yourself and hang in there, even when challenges arise. You don't have to say "Oh, screw it," back off and sell yourself short again. You can push through the difficulty. You can achieve something, even if it is less than you wanted or expected to. You don't have to leave school because you got a B or a C grade. You can't always get A's. Sometimes you have to adjust your expectations of yourself and learn to take smaller steps forward.

Chances are, you have felt like a failure because you have set impossibly high standards for yourself. Now you can set realistic standards and more modest goals. Every time you reach one of those goals, you will be building your confidence. Winning many small victories may not seem glamorous to you, but those victories add up and before long you may be closer to manifesting your dreams than you realize.

Babies learn to crawl before they walk, and they learn to walk before they run. Adults are not so smart. They expect to go from the cradle to the high-wire. They set themselves up for failure.

Spiritual Law number four tells us about the importance of practicing and taking small, concrete steps toward our goal. We don't become a master until we have completed our apprenticeship. We can't skip over steps.

If you have tried to skip steps in the past and have fallen on your face, don't despair. Just take the time to go back and touch those bases. Complete your apprenticeship so that you can move on.

Don't be afraid to be a student. Don't look down on the preparation stage. It is what gives you the confidence and strength to teach and to perform. You can't be a leader if you have never learned to follow one. You need mentors and teachers that inspire you if you are going to develop your full potential.

I don't know any lion tamers who wanted to get in the ring with the lion until they had finished all their lion taming classes. Why would you want to be the exception to the rule?

When you have confidence in yourself and your skills are solid and reliable, then you can say goodbye to your teacher. Then you are prepared to learn on your own and develop your own unique talents. Then you too will be on the road to mastery.

Everyone who practices diligently eventually realizes his talent and fulfills his calling. The best students always surpass their teachers' abilities. And then it is time for them to mentor and teach the next generation.

The Difference between a Job and a Calling

There is a difference between a job and a calling. A job is something you do to survive. There is a certain dignity involved in supporting yourself and in helping to support others. You can become a skilled worker and feel a legitimate pride in your abilities. You can pat yourself on the back for buying your spouse a new car and sending your kids to college. However, suppose your boss comes to you and says: "Listen, John or Sally, we appreciate your efforts, and we are going to keep paying you your salary, but we now have a robot that can do your job better than you can. So it won't be necessary for you to come to work anymore. We'll just put your check in the mail every other Friday."

Are you going to argue with him or say "Great. Thanks a lot."

If it's just a job you are doing, you are going to say "Thanks" and hit the golf course or the beach. But if it's a calling, you aren't going to accept being fired. "What do you mean?" you'll ask. "This is my calling. I have to do it. There isn't any question about it, so please don't argue with me. I'll just come here every day and make sure the robot does the job right!"

A calling is something you choose to do because it is an expression of who you are. It enables you to realize your talents and abilities. It gives you joy and brings joy to others. You can quit your job, but you can't quit your calling. Even if you take a break from it for a year or two, you will come back to it before long.

It is your calling because it helps you give your gift. It helps you give back to others what you have learned most deeply and profoundly in your life. It is the area not just where you are skilled, but where you have achieved mastery.

Others know this and seek you out. Even if you don't list your phone number in the phonebook and refuse to advertise your abilities, word will still get out and people will find their way to your doorstep.

It isn't easy to resign from your calling. That is because it is your spiritual purpose. It is why you are here.

Practice 7 B

Trusting Your Calling

During the week, take some time to consider what your calling is. What are your greatest talents, abilities, and sensitivities? Is there something that you do that gives you joy and inspires others? Are you finding ways to express your gifts? If not, what is holding you back?

Use the information in this chapter to look at any fears or blocks that are preventing you from getting in touch with your life purpose and/or acting on it. Then, see if you can take a few concrete steps this week to walk through those fears or to remove those blocks.

Take small risks if you are afraid to take bigger ones. Admit your fears and anxieties to yourself and others, but don't let them hold you back.

If you have adopted a career to try to please others, ask yourself "Do I know what I *really* want to be doing? Do I want to go through my whole life living out someone else's dream, instead of my own?"

This week, question any role that is not in alignment with your life purpose and get in touch with your fear of failure or fear of success. This week, let yourself experience the joy of authentic self expression. Let yourself be called to your calling. Trust yourself, trust your gift and find a way to express it.

The Difference between a Skill and Mastery

A skill is something that you learn. You are not born with it. You have to learn to be a carpenter or a plumber. You are not born with these skills.

Most people who work hard and have reasonable ability can learn a skill. But to become masters, they have to have another ingredient. They have to have talent.

Talent is something you are born with. For example, great eye-hand coordination is a talent. Those who are born with it have the potential of mastering a variety of skills. Depending on their other talents, interests and the training available to them, they might become master carpenters, surgeons, or violinists.

There are as many talents as there are expressions of the physical or psychic senses. A person with emotional sensitivity to plants or animals might become a celebrated gardener or veterinarian. A person with a great sense of design or color might become a painter or interior decorator. A person with a strong ability to feel through her hands might become a potter or a healer.

Mastery requires both talent and training (skill development). One might come into this life with the capacity to become a great pianist, but potential by itself is not enough. One must find teachers/mentors and begin to practice. The more skilled one becomes, the more talented his teachers or mentors must be if he is to keep developing his talent.

Great students require great teachers. And great teachers are generally interested only in working with students who have outstanding talent and commitment.

Practice 7 C

Identify Your Opportunities to Learn, Perform or Teach

During the week, take some time to identify the specific talents and abilities you were born with and to consider how you have developed these talents in your life so far. Have you taken the time to get the training you need to develop your talents to their full potential? If not, can you commit to doing so? What are the opportunities available to you for learning? Who are your potential teachers or mentors? Please take concrete steps this week to address these questions.

If you have already developed your proficiency, are you ready to say goodbye to your teachers and move out on your own? Are you ready to perform or to teach?

Performing gives you a direct connection with an audience or a client base. It enables you to share your talent and dazzle others with your skill. It is doing what you do best. It empowers you and inspires others.

Teaching enables you to pass along your wisdom and skill to the next generation. It empowers others to trust their gifts and to shine.

Some performers do not make good teachers. They need the spotlight. They inspire others through their example, but they are not patient enough to teach. On the other hand, some teachers do not enjoy performing or simply are not good at it. But they take delight in empowering others.

Some people like to be out on stage. Others prefer to work behind the scenes helping to stage the production.

What role works best for you? Is it your strength to work as a performer or as a teacher? Do you want to be on stage or working in a support capacity? Or do you do both equally well?

During the week, record your answers to these and related questions in your journal. Share any insights you receive with friends and colleagues, and act on any opportunity you have to play the role that best suits you.

Getting Off the Cross of Perfection

There are two ways to measure our progress in life. One is to measure our achievements against those of others. The other is to measure our progress in relationship to where we started.

When we measure our achievements against those of others (the competitive model) we can easily feel disappointed. Generally there will be others who will have achieved a higher level of mastery than we have.

At any given time in any given category, you can have only one champion of the world. If you are highly competitive, you may feel like a failure if you fall short of winning the championship.

Those who have exceedingly high standards are asking for trouble. If you spend your entire life trying to win a marathon, you aren't going to be happy coming in number 50, even if the field numbers 100. But if you just started running a year ago, being number 50 isn't such a slap in the face. That's how relative all these measurements are.

In the competitive model, success and failure seem to be determined by some objective measure, but that is rarely the case. Success and failure are entirely subjective. They depend more often than not on the expectations you have and how high your standards are.

There are two ways to be successful if you believe in the competitive model. One is: *do a little bit better next time.* The other is: *lower your expectations.* Then, you won't be disappointed if you come in number 40 or 45 next year.

Of course, the competitive model has its limitations, even when you try to massage it or modify it. You can decrease the weight of the cross, but you will still be carrying it.

If you want to put the cross down, you need to drop the competitive model completely and stop measuring your skills in relationship to those of others.

This is a far more gentle process.

You can still set goals and make steady progress toward them. You can improve, become proficient, even achieve mastery. Then, winning or losing a competition isn't the only measure of your success. Other measures are more important, such as "Did I play better today than I did last week or last month?" or "Did I play as well as I could?"

With more integral measures such as this, we can lose a competition and still feel good about ourselves and about our performance. We can also feel good about the person who beat us.

It isn't surprising that a gracious loser wins big in the hearts of an audience. Humility is a necessary ingredient in real success.

Everyone wants to win. Everyone wants to be the best. But there can be only one champion of the world and most of the time that is not going to be you or me.

But who is the real champion: the one who wins or the one who accepts the decision, whatever it is, with dignity and grace?

Winning is only one small component in the making of a champion. A real champion is a gracious loser and a humble winner. He does not try to make himself look good at the expense of his opponent. He does not gloat after a victory, no matter how significant it is, but instead praises his opponent and expresses gratitude for the match.

Winners who behave badly are not champions, even if they call themselves champs. They are poor role models for our children and they bring shame and disrespect to their craft or their sport.

A Land Beyond Failure

Those who feel that they have failed because they have made serious mistakes or lost an important competition have not only lost touch with their creative essence; they have become caught in the barbed wire of their own rigid standards.

They need to change their standards and expectations and learn to be gentle with themselves.

Some of the most successful people in the world have failed miserably at something they tried to do. But instead of allowing their failure to derail them, they chose to learn from their mistakes and to renew their commitment to their goal.

Indeed, it is unlikely that one can really succeed until he or she learns how to fail.

Little kids who are learning how to walk take some nasty falls. But in time they learn how to brace themselves so that those falls don't hurt as much. And because they are persistent they eventually develop the motor skills they need to stand up on two legs and take their first few steps.

I don't think that learning to run a company or a country is any different. Great leaders not only fail; they learn profound lessons from their mistakes so that they don't repeat them. They make their lemons into lemonade and before we know it we are raising our glasses to toast them.

A great boxer has to be able to take a great punch. He might even have to be knocked out once or twice to come back with the skill and intensity he is capable of.

We don't tell him he has to retire if he gets hit or knocked out. We applaud when he comes back. That is because we know that you can't really win until you have lost and know what that is like.

In America, we root for the little guy. We inevitably choose David over Goliath. We cheer for the underdog.

Have you ever wondered why?

It doesn't do much for anyone to see the big brute win the fight. He might be stronger, but we don't like him.

In the end, we like our heroes to be human beings like us. We like the fact that Abe Lincoln became president. We like the fact that some day, perhaps against the odds, we might be the one to shine.

Every human being on the planet has a talent and a calling. We don't have to measure his talent against someone else's. His talent is important in and of itself.

If you are having a pot luck, one person brings the meat, another person brings the potatoes, someone else brings the salad, or the wine or the dessert. And when everyone finally assembles around the table, a genuine feast is born. Everyone benefits from what everyone else brings.

That is why we must be committed to the creative process,

not just for a select few, but for each person on the planet. That is why we must support and empower every human being to discover his or her gifts and to offer them to the world.

We cannot achieve our potential as a nation or as a species until all of us are empowered and all of our gifts have been brought forward. Then, the table of life will overflow with abundant offerings and the real feast can begin. I like to think of this as the *First Supper* of the New Paradigm.

Jesus had the *Last Supper* of the Old Paradigm. The gifts that were brought to the table then could not be tasted in this world. They had to be promised in the next.

But when the entire human family gathers around the table of life, when no one is ostracized or left out, we will finally experience what true abundance means. Each gift that is brought will be as important as another. Each dish will feed someone, even if the person who brought it knows not for whom he cooked the food, or if the person who eats it has no idea why he likes it.

We don't have to know why we have our gift. We simply need to understand it, nurture it, and bring it forth. Until it has been received, we cannot know the full extent of its value or meaning.

Being the Best We can Be

The army has a slogan that promises its enlistees that it will enable them to "be the best they can be." That slogan should be adopted by every school, every prison, every nursing home, every institution in our society that is attempting to help people.

This is the language of empowerment. It is the language of the New Paradigm.

We don't have to be better than others. We just need to be the best we can be.

When we go beyond winning and losing, beyond comparison or competition, when we go to the core, the heart of the matter, we know that everyone has a gift and that gift is exactly what is needed by the world. Our job is to nurture that gift in every human being.

Our salvation depends on it.

Results of the Seventh Spiritual Practice

This week's practice helps us transform our experience of:

Rigid perfectionism and inordinately high standards for ourselves and others

Unworthiness, lack of faith and trust in ourselves and the universe

Inability to express ourselves and take risks

Self criticism and inordinate fear of the criticism of others

Poverty and scarcity consciousness

Fear of failure and fear of success

Underachievement or overachievement

Settling for a job instead of being open to manifesting our life purpose and our calling

Struggle

It helps us develop and/or experience:

Realistic standards and expectations as well as patience with our mistakes and those of others

Self worth, trust in ourselves and in the universe

Willingness to take risks and open to new experiences

Willingness to listen to constructive criticism

Abundance and generosity

Resilience, ability to learn from our mistakes or failures

Achievement, success

Commitment to our life purpose and our calling

Grace

SUMMARY OF PRACTICE: *If you need to work on perfectionism, cultivate unconditional self-worth. Ease up on yourself and others. If you need to work on procrastination or fear of failure, learn how to accept feedback from teachers and mentors so that you can develop your skills. Step forward; trust your talents and gifts and risk sharing them with others.*

The Power of Healing

The Eighth Spiritual Practice

Sooner or later, when we ignore our gifts and instead focus on doing what other people want us to do, we either fail or we get depressed. In this case, outright failure is usually a blessing, because it wakes us up and forces us to realize that we need to make changes in our priorities.

Often we get sick or injured or our relationships fall apart for the same reason. Our lives are out of balance and it is time for a wake up call.

Most of us get used to doing things a certain way. Our lives are on automatic pilot. We get into a pattern and before long it becomes a rut that we can't dig out of.

Unhealthy habits and addictive behavior rob us of our flexibility and resilience. They block our connection to our spiritual center and disconnect us from our creative energies. When we are experiencing physical, emotional or mental rigidity, we often need a crisis to unlock our frozen energy and help us reconnect to who we really are.

Perhaps we get fired from our job or get into a car accident on the way to work. Life says to us "Stop. This won't work any more. It's time to change."

We might hate the act that slows us down or forces us to take notice. We might feel sorry for ourselves or get angry at God for this apparent slap in the face. We might kick and scream for a while.

But if and when we get over it, if and when we accept our lives the way they are and begin to pick up the pieces, we realize that we have been given a precious gift. We have been given a chance to get off the merry-go-round and remember what it is that we came into this life to do.

That is the "Ahah" moment when we understand and commit to our spiritual purpose. Now we don't have to spin our wheels any more. Our direction is clear. We just need to put one foot in front of the other.

The number eight is about death and rebirth; it is about transformation. It is symbolized by the phoenix being reborn from the ashes of destruction. It is a time of emotional turmoil and psychological adjustment. There may even be physical pain.

But eight is also symbolized by the caterpillar emerging from his cocoon as a butterfly. The old self has died and the new self has found its wings.

Personal and Collective Healing

Until we experience such a healing crisis in our lives, we may be narrow and selfish. We believe that we are here to take care of ourselves only. But after our healing crisis, we know that our healing is intimately connected to the healing of others. We have no choice but to share our experience with others when they ask us to. And we don't need to be reimbursed or recognized for sharing our gift.

All great movements of healing happen in this way, through

love and spontaneous sharing. The gift is never withheld from anyone who asks for it.

This may be a ministry of sorts, but it has no dogma or denomination and preaching is not allowed. It is not about trying to save those who don't want to be saved.

There is no trespass in this. One does not try to cram the gift down anyone's throat. One offers the gift only to those who want it.

It is about meeting the need. It is about feeding the hungry, healing the sick, loving those who need to be loved.

Spiritual Law Number Eight is about healing, not just for the individual, but for all human beings, for all plants and animals, for the entire planet. It is about bringing balance to that which has gone out of balance; it is about bringing that which has gone astray back on track.

It is about redemption and forgiveness.

One does not find that in a vacuum. One does not heal alone, but with others.

In the early Christian communities, people came together to offer each other forgiveness. Rituals of absolution were open to all. Often, one had to come and experience how others forgave to know that forgiveness was possible for oneself.

So understand that your healing is connected to the healing of others. If you are trying to heal alone, you are taking an unnecessarily difficult journey. Someone who has gone before you can help show you the way. And when you have healed, you can reach back and help another through the doorway.

My teacher told me: "I am the Door to Love Without Conditions. When you walk through you will also be the door."

One is not a healer by virtue of some special privilege; one is a healer by virtue of one's own experience and willingness to share it with others.

Let me tell you something you don't want to hear. Until you walk through the door, you cannot be your brother's keeper, because you yourself have not healed. But once you have passed through the doorway, once you have healed, it is your responsibility and your calling to help others who are coming behind you.

When you have healed, you are your brother's keeper. You are responsible not just for yourself, but for everyone who appears at your doorstep.

Someone like Jesus or Buddha knows this. They know they have to feed everyone who comes to their table. They wouldn't even think about turning anyone away.

Building your House of Healing

In 1935, Bill W. was on a business trip in Akron, Ohio. He had not touched a drop of alcohol for six months, but things had not gone well in his business and alone, away from home, and feeling depressed, Bill W. was sorely tempted to reach for a bottle. He knew that he needed to find another alcoholic to help him stay sober. Fortunately Bill W. was guided to Dr. Bob, another recovering alcoholic. That meeting between two recovering alcoholics in Akron, Ohio was the beginning of Alcoholics Anonymous.

The secret to their success was simple. It took one brother in pain to understand and help another in pain.

It took four years for the first 100 alcoholics in the first three groups to get sober. Then *The Twelve Steps of Alcoholics Anonymous* was published. Publicity made the work more widely known and one of the greatest Healing Houses in modern time was established.

In 1967, my friend Elisabeth Kübler Ross began teaching a series of weekly seminars on death and dying to medical students at the University of Chicago's Billings Hospital. As part of her teaching, she interviewed many dying patients. Her book *On Death and Dying*, published in 1969, was based on these interviews. The book became a bestseller and helped to change attitudes toward death and dying in the medical community as well as in the general public. In 1974, the first hospices in the US were founded, providing dying people with support and a place to die in dignity.

Today, there are over 2500 hospices in the US. Indeed the hospice movement has transformed the way we look at death and dying in western culture. Before Elisabeth heard the call, death and dying were taboo subjects and most people died in hospital settings without love, support or compassion. They died alone with no one to talk to about their fears, their guilt, or their suffering.

Elisabeth recognized the need. She walked through that doorway and, because of that, she helped to build one of the great Houses of Healing in recent history.

Both AA and the hospice movement drew their strength and integrity from volunteers who put their hearts and souls into helping others. They created environments where human beings gave without strings attached to other human beings.

Why are there so few examples like this?

Many public institutions are meant to be Houses of Healing. Prisons, schools, hospitals and clinics, nursing homes, shelters for battered women or the homeless, even welfare or unemployment offices, are all supposed to be places where people are helping other people transform their lives.

Instead, these institutions are bureaucracies where mismanagement and waste are common and caring and compassion are rare. Transformation and redemption, when it does happen for individuals, often happens in spite of organizational efforts and not because of them.

Institutions do not create a culture of atonement and forgiveness. People do. And real redemption happens best in an environment staffed by people who have overcome similar hardships and transformed their lives.

To put it simply, government is not going to build the Houses of Healing that are necessary in your community and mine. And it is highly unlikely that churches, temples or synagogues are going to build them, especially if they are going to be open to people with different backgrounds and beliefs.

No, if the Houses of Healing are to be built, you and I will have to build them, just as Bill W., Dr. Bob and Elisabeth Kübler-Ross did.

To build your House of Healing, you must be willing to serve. You must feel compassion for others whose needs are not being met. The suffering of others must touch your heart.

Sometimes that happens because, like Bill W., you have experienced a certain type of suffering and can reach out and help others who are going through the same thing. Your House of Healing is discovered as you seek healing for your own wound.

The Houses of Healing are places of empowerment and transformation. They are places where people can feel love and support, heal their wounds individually and in small groups, and rebuild their lives with greater authenticity. They are places where the old dies and the new is born.

There are as many Houses of Healing as there are wounds that must be healed. If you have recovered from sexual abuse or a cult experience, your House of Healing helps you and others understand and heal through these experiences. If you lose a loved one to cancer or AIDS, your House of Healing might involve working with others who have the same disease or raising money to support research into a potential cure.

Practice 8 A

Discovering your House of Healing

Take the following three steps to discover your House of Healing.

1. Identify your own wound and ask yourself how you can take the next step in your own healing.
2. Identify the people whose wounds and unmet needs speak most clearly and deeply to your heart.
3. Identify your talent or your gift and consider how you might share your gift in addressing the area of healing you identified in steps 1 and 2. Record your insights in your journal.

Your willingness is all that matters. When you are ready to step more deeply into your own healing and help others heal, the call will come. It might not be the one you expect it to be, but be open to it, whatever form it takes.

Elisabeth Kübler Ross was not planning to teach classes on death and dying to medical students. She was asked and she said "Yes." The same might happen to you. An opportunity for which you are uniquely suited may arise and take you completely by surprise.

Don't say "No" to it. Explore the possibilities.

Perhaps you don't feel qualified to do what you are being asked to do. That happens to a lot of us. But don't stop there. Ask yourself, "Am I willing to do it?" Do I think it is important and am I willing to put my best energy into it? Can I be committed to what I am asked to do?

If the answer to these questions is "Yes," then the fact that you have little or no prior experience should not be the deciding factor. Perhaps your lack of experience is an asset. Perhaps it will enable you to look at the challenge before you in a new way.

Some of us know exactly what our House of Healing is. We know where to go and who to talk to.

Others of us have no idea. But life opens a door before us and, because we are open and willing, we walk through it, not knowing that we are going to step into our life purpose.

Your spiritual practice this week is to identify or be open to discovering your House of Healing. If you have not healed from some long-standing addiction or wound, don't stay in denial. Come clean and ask for help.

If you have healed from your wound or addiction, reach out to others who can benefit from your help. Helping others is a profound way of maintaining your own health and well being, as Alcoholics Anonymous and other Twelve Step programs have overwhelmingly demonstrated.

Those who belong to your House of Healing have healing needs that are similar to your own. Your job is to find them and embrace them.

During this week be conscious of the fact that you are helping to create a culture of healing and forgiveness for yourself and others. If there are role models who can guide you and programs that inspire you, do not hesitate to connect with them. But if there is nothing available, don't despair. This is a sign that you are here to be a pioneer.

You are being called to tread where perhaps only angels have tread before you. While the human side of you may shrink before the challenge and feel unworthy or incapable of answering the call, your true Self knows that you have no choice.

Your healing depends on stepping forward and becoming visible and vulnerable.

If you do not step forward and acknowledge your pain, not only will you not heal, but hundreds, perhaps even thousands who share your wound, won't find their pathway to healing.

That's why you can't say "No" to the call when it comes. You have to say "Yes," even if you are scared or anxious. Your healing belongs not just to you. It belongs to all of us.

Practice 8 B

Establish a Weekly Meeting for Mutual Healing and Support

If you have not yet established a weekly healing and support group now is the time to do so. Here is how to begin:

1. Having identified your wound, articulate where you are in your healing process to at least one other person with similar needs.

2. Ask for the support of others in your community who have the same or a similar wound.

3. Gather together with these people, share where you are in your healing journey and invite others to do the same. Be specific about areas where you need help from others and areas where you might be able to offer help. (Follow the communications guidelines in my book *Living In the Heart* so that a safe space can be created and maintained).

4. Begin meeting weekly with this group of people and work together to reach out to others in your community who can assist you and/or benefit from your efforts.

Remember, while each person's healing requires his or her individual commitment, for which there can be no substitute, it also makes a profound social statement, offering others hope that there is a way out of their suffering. The healing of any individual sends a message to all. That is why our willingness to stand up and own our addiction, our wound, or our disease and to tell the story of our healing empowers others to leave their isolation and hopelessness behind.

How many of us have the opportunity to speak a truth that helps to set others free? How many of us are willing to go up on the stage of life and give our testimony?

For those on the spiritual path, there is no choice. When the bell sounds, we need to mount the steps. We know in every cell of our bodies that we will rise up and let our voice be heard, for it is what we came to do. We are simply fulfilling our destiny.

Results of the Eighth Spiritual Practice

This week's practice helps us overcome the following limitations:

Denial of our wound and our need to heal from it
Lack of a community that supports and empowers us
Intensification of our own suffering and that of others
Inability to move forward in creating our House of
   Healing and discovering our life purpose

This week's practice helps us to:

Acknowledge our wound and ask for help in healing it
Find a healing community where love and support are
   given and received
Bring balance back into our lives
Discover the gift we have to offer to others

SUMMARY OF PRACTICE: *Understand where you need to heal and discover your House of Healing. Meet with others who share a wound and a healing journey similar to your own.*

The Power of Individuation
The Ninth Spiritual Practice

For one who has mounted the stage to tell his story, the limelight can be intoxicating. One can become attached to the applause and the approval. One can be attached to one's public role, to being an icon or an inspiration to others. The great danger for us and for those whom we wish to inspire is that our words will cease to be heartfelt and become stale and predictable. Instead of dropping our images of self and moving to the cutting edge of our growth, where our lessons lie, we may cling to who we think we are or to who we think others want or expect us to be.

One who is addicted to telling the story of his healing probably does not believe it. Yet he is afraid to retire from the public stage to face whatever demons may still lurk in the shadows of his consciousness. He pretends to have completed his healing process when life is calling him to a deeper and more profound healing.

Others feel that something is not quite right, but they do not know what it is, until he stumbles and falls. And then he suffers far worse pain and humiliation than he would have suffered if he had been more honest with himself and others.

We all know a few spiritual teachers or other leaders who have fallen from their pedestals. In one way or another, they have refused to hear the inner call for healing and have betrayed the trust that was placed in them.

The Ninth Spiritual Law shows us the "Emperors who have no clothes." It exposes deception, hypocrisy, and the abuse of power. Those who do not walk their talk are inevitably seen for what they are and humbled.

The Right Use of Power

The right use of power is to actualize Self and empower others. Those who achieve spiritual mastery become self-realized human beings. They have the power of uniqueness; they are one-of-a-kind expressions of All That Is. Having become all that they can be, they can empower others to fulfill their own potential.

They help others to stand as equals. Thus, they uphold the spiritual law of equality. They know that every human being has a unique and important gift that must be nurtured and brought forth. And they do all they can as midwives and facilitators to help people find the inner light and let it shine.

But one who is attached to being the leader, the teacher, or the authority figure is incapable of realizing self or empowering others. In order to do either, he must drop his attachment to name and fame, power and position and attend to his own healing. He must surrender his spiritual pride and cultivate humility. He must learn to be in the world, but not of the world.

Worldly power and position do not last forever. Leaders and authority figures rise and fall, come in and out of favor. Famous athletes or movie stars rise to the heights of popularity only to experience public indifference or disgrace.

There is a huge difference between outer authority and inner authority. Outer authority is power or influence over others. Inner authority is the power that comes from being authentic and true to oneself.

Outer authority comes appropriately perhaps at a certain stage in one's life. But it must also be relinquished when it ceases to be timely or appropriate.

One must lay the scepter down when one can no longer be effective as a leader. To retire from the public eye or from a prominent position is a natural thing. No one who comes into power holds onto it forever.

The wise person accepts power when it comes to her and she knows that she can use it effectively, and she surrenders it when it becomes clear that she no longer has the support and backing of others.

Stepping down, detaching, retiring can be an act of grace or we can resist the inevitable and humiliate ourselves.

A great basketball player is a superstar for only part of his career. In the beginning he is honing his skills, learning the ropes, and moving toward mastery. In the end, he begins to realize that others can contribute as much or perhaps even more than he can. So, if he is wise and in touch with the truth, he accepts a different role on the team and plays fewer minutes.

However, if he is in denial about his abilities, he tries to hold on. He starts when he should be sitting on the bench. He tries to accomplish what he used to be able to do and gets frustrated, tired, even angry at himself and his teammates. He does not know how to let go, how to detach, how to surrender.

Detaching

The number nine is about detachment and relinquishing our burdens. It is about the freedom and grace that arise when we lighten our load and let go of responsibilities that have been fulfilled.

The great challenge for those who have achieved some kind of worldly mastery is to break their attachment to the role of leader, teacher, or healer. They are used to being needed by others. They are used to having people come to them and ask for guidance or advice.

It isn't easy to stop being the person who has the answers. It isn't easy to say: "My time to advise and lead is over. I am sure that you will find the answers for yourself or find another teacher to help you."

One takes a major step toward spiritual mastery when one can let go of the role and responsibility of teaching others. A spiritual master is not attached to the role that he plays. He can be teacher or student. He can be president of the board or janitor. He knows that his worth is not dependent on what he does, the position that he has, or the role that he plays.

And so she stops giving the answers and speaks simply for herself. She regains her spiritual center and anchors herself in her own experience. She spends time alone, perhaps in retreat from the world, not in an attempt to run away, for she has shown that she can be successful in the world, but rather as an attempt to find a deeper center and clearer vision of her life as it is now.

She surrenders the past. She stops living for the future. She enters the present naked and empty.

The time comes for all of us when it is good and right to simplify our lives and pare down our duties and responsibilities. We don't need to head for a monastery or a mountain cave to detach from the incessant demands of life.

We can simplify and detach where we are. When people come to the door and ask for a counseling session or an evening talk, we can say: "Thank you for asking, but this is a time when I wish to be quiet."

The real relinquishment happens not outwardly but inwardly. We do not need to wear a loin cloth and sell our car to be free of the stress of money and possessions. But we can find a way to lessen the time we spend thinking about or attending to these things.

The movement within to the core of our being is a return to our essence. It is also an acceptance of our uniqueness as human beings. We are content simply to be who we are moment-to-moment. The desire to live in reference to others simply drops away.

When we accept ourselves completely, others don't push our buttons very much. We have little desire to change, fix or reform others. So the drama may continue around us, but we are watching it, rather than playing it out.

The tendency to project onto others, positively or negatively, drops away. Only spiritual relationships of honesty and mutual respect are possible as we sink into the core of our being.

Ironically, we enter into the universal experience not by trying to be like others, but by being ourselves fully. Shadow and persona fuse together. The capacity for both good and evil rest within us as a palpable moment-to-moment reality.

Who needs outer gods and demons, heroes and villains when s/he knows that all the opposites of human experience rest within consciousness? Dark and light, high and low, left and right meet and come to balance in our own psyches. And when that happens duality consciousness begins to rest in something greater than itself. It rests in Oneness. Here, everyone and everything is acceptable and loveable just as it is.

We call it individuation when the individual becomes who he really is, and makes his peace with his brothers and sisters. He no longer has any battles to fight or wrongs to right.

He is content being exactly where he is. That means what he does or where he goes does not matter greatly anymore. He will rest in the same consciousness regardless of his orientation in time or space.

Thus, most of what the world strives for no longer has meaning for him. He lives now simply to be himself fully, which takes no effort.

This is true freedom and true detachment. Because he is centered in himself, he moves spontaneously in the flow of life and not against it. Like the old Taoist masters, he comes and goes freely without deliberation or struggle.

Practice 9

Seven Day Spiritual Retreat

Your spiritual practice this week is to go on a full-time spiritual retreat. If possible, attend one of our Spiritual Mastery retreats. Otherwise, find a retreat center that will meet your needs and use the following guidelines to design your own retreat.

1. Cultivate inner vision and inner authority.
2. Detach from external power and authority.
3. Spend time alone in retreat and solitude.
4. Listen deeply and live from the inside out.
5. Think, feel and speak from your essence; otherwise, be empty and silent.
6. Remove external stimulation. (No TV, radio, newspapers, movies, etc.)
7. Let go of all agendas. Be aware of your breath, and be present in everything that you do.
8. Do not try to have any experience.
9. Don't resist any experience that arises spontaneously.
10. Stay in the present. Let past and future go.

Imagine that you are God and you just finished creating the world. It is the end of the sixth day and night. Now, as the seventh day dawns, it is time to rest and reflect on what you have created.

During the Sabbath, we rest in the arms of our Creator. This week is a Sabbath week for you.

Unlike other times when doing "more" is better, this week the "less" you do the better. So if possible, don't ride in a car. Don't drink, smoke, take drugs or engage in sexual activity alone or with others. Fast or eat less than you normally do. Talk less (keep conversations short and sweet) or take a vow of silence for the week. If possible, refrain from reading or even journalling. Your focus this week is to be internal rather than external.

That doesn't mean that you have to close your eyes. However, don't become attached or involved in what your eyes see. Just be present.

As you go through the week, reflect on the themes of detachment, simplifying your life, surrendering external authority and outer power and accepting inner authority and the call to authenticity. Ask yourself what roles and images of self are excess baggage now and begin to let them go.

The ninth spiritual practice gives you a chance to deepen your daily practice of God Communion and take it to a whole new level. If you have been doing the spiritual practices in this book faithfully for the last eight weeks, then you will be ready for this week of spiritual retreat. If not, you might want to revisit some of the previous practices and schedule your retreat later. Keep in mind that the optimum time for a spiritual retreat is few days before and a few days after the new moon.

Results of the Ninth Spiritual Practice

This week's practice helps us overcome the following limitations:

Inappropriate use of power or position

Spiritual pride

Attachment to the pedestal, the throne, or the podium

Complexity in thinking and lifestyle

Inappropriate commitments, investment in roles that no longer serve us or others

Need to control self or others

Our practice this week encourages us to:

Cultivate inner authority; surrender outer authority

Cultivate humility

Lay down our burdens and simplify our lives
Let go of roles and responsibilities that no longer serve us
 or others
Release ourselves and others from any commitments we
 cannot keep
Set ourselves and others free

SUMMARY OF PRACTICE: *Attend one of our Spiritual Mastery retreats or find a retreat center and spend seven consecutive days intensifying your spiritual practice.*

The Power of Transcendence

The Tenth Spiritual Practice

When I was a kid, I remember a song the lyrics of which went something like this:

First there was a mountain;
Then there was no mountain;
Then there was.

When we embark on the spiritual path, we see the mountain clearly and plainly. Then, after years of meditation and other spiritual practice, the mountain seems to disappear into thin air. However, just when we are about to puff ourselves up, thinking we have accomplished some major spiritual feat, the mountain reappears.

We can't really make the mountain go away. We can't avoid the challenges and uncertainties of life. But we can change our reactive stance toward them. We can change the way we perceive what happens to us.

Another way of saying this is "Before enlightenment, we have to chop wood and carry water . . . . After enlightenment, we have to chop wood and carry water." But we don't chop or carry in the same way.

Enlightenment is not some kind of magic that changes our external situation. It is a shift out of duality consciousness into

Unity Consciousness. It enables us to see ourselves and others as we truly are.

Flashes of light or Unity Consciousness happen throughout our life. They intensify as we individuate and realize our true Self.

Individuation may bring us to the door between the human world and the divine world. Enlightenment takes us across the threshold. In Enlightenment the small self dissolves into the larger Self and the personal dissolves into the Universal.

When Jesus becomes the Christ or Gautama becomes the Buddha, they leave the personal behind and are absorbed into the Universal. They become one with God or All That Is. When that happens, the men we called Jesus and Gautama no longer exist. All that remains is Christ and Buddha.

This experience is characterized by the death or relinquishment of ego consciousness. There is no more will to survive at any cost, nor is there a fear of death or attachment to the physical body. As the Self is realized, one's sense of separateness from other human beings and life forms gradually dissolves. When enlightenment occurs, all experiences of separation come to an end and one transcends the limitations of physical experience.

The light experienced at the moment of enlightenment is experienced by every person who dies. For what dies is not the light within, but all that shrouds or disguises the light. When we die, all that is false falls away from us. Only truth or light remains.

Our last experience in the human body is that blaze or starburst of the light that has been inside us. It literally explodes in our consciousness as the body takes its last breath. That explosion of light is the liberation of our Spirit from its containment in form.

Those who experience enlightenment do not have to wait for

physical death to experience this moment of release and liberation. They experience it while still living in the body.

However, after this experience, their connection to the body remains tenuous and they often have great difficulty staying in the world. Only those who live close to this place can understand them or care for them.

Practice 10

Be In the World but not Of the World

When you went on your seven day spiritual retreat last week you may have had flashes of light, moments of bliss, times when the boundaries between the outer world and the inner world seemed to fade. Perhaps the mountain seemed for a while to disappear.

But now you have returned to your life and you are faced with the same cares and responsibilities you had when you left. The mountain remains and looks back at you.

The question then is not: "How can I escape from the world so that I can go back into bliss?" but "How can I be blissful in the world?" or as Jesus asked "How can I be in the world but not of the world?"

When you open to love, you begin to see through the eyes of love. Seen through the eyes of love, that mountain of cares and responsibilities looks very different than it does when it is seen through the eyes of fear.

Returning to the world, your challenge is to see it through the eyes of love. You are asked to be present in your life without being attached to any particular outcome. You are asked to live simply, honestly, authentically, without being drawn into the drama.

As you return to your home, your community, your job, remember to keep things simple. When you awaken each day know that God is All there is. Be gentle with your fear and that of others and remember that fear arises only when you forget who you are.

As you remember the truth about you and others, life will seem more dream than drama. You will float in and out of the dream, sometimes lucid, sometimes not, but without getting attached to what is happening there.

After all, a dream is just a dream. And you are not just the one who comes and goes in the dream, but the dreamer himself or herself.

Results of the Tenth Spiritual Practice

This week's practice helps us break through our:

Attachment to the drama of life and the roles that we play
Tendency to live in the past or future
Tendency to see life through our judgments and fears
Tendency to perceive problems and the need to fix them
Expectations of rewards or outcomes
Condemnation of ourselves and others for mistakes and
    trespasses

It helps us remember to:

Detach from the drama
Stay in the present
See through the eyes of acceptance and love
Recognize what isn't broken and doesn't need to be fixed
Give and receive without conditions or expectations
Offer forgiveness to everyone, including ourselves

SUMMARY OF PRACTICE: *Simplify your life. Be in the world, but not of the world.*

Epilogue

Congratulations. You have completed the experiential curriculum of *The Power of Love*.

I hope that you have had a direct experience of the power of love operating in your life during the last ten weeks and that you will continue the elements of this practice that you have found helpful.

These experiential practices are not meant to be performed for a week and then forgotten. They are meant to be integrated into the fabric of your life.

Toward that end, many of you will benefit from repeating this experiential curriculum at another time—or perhaps even many times—in your life. If you rushed through the exercises this time, try to slow down your pace the next time you work with these practices. Take two weeks or a month for each spiritual practice. That way you can practice at depth.

If you have not read the companion volume *The Laws of Love: A Guide to Living in Harmony with Universal Spiritual Truth,* you may find it helpful to read that book or listen to the CD workshop series by the same title the next time you undertake these practices. Ideally, each Law should be studied at the same time that one engages in the corresponding Spiritual Practice.

If you feel drawn to this material and would like to study and practice it on a deeper level, you can purchase the third book in the series entitled *The Presence of Love: Advanced Principles and*

Practices. You can also talk with us about attending a spiritual retreat and enrolling in our teacher certification program.

May the light that is in you shine forth and illumine your journey, now and for each moment of your life.

Namaste.

Paul Ferrini

A Note on Teacher Certification

Paul Ferrini will be providing ongoing training for people who find this material helpful and would like to learn to teach it to others.

The Laws of Love book and CD series present the intellectual underpinning and structure for the spiritual practices offered in this book. All candidates for teacher certification are asked to study *The Laws of Love* in depth, in addition to completing the ten week experiential practice program and keeping a daily journal.

Level 1 certification enables one to teach a two hour introductory version of this material. Level 2 certification enables one to teach the full 20 hour Laws of Love course.

Certification candidates will have the possibility of earning a living as full time teachers and going on to become spiritual counselors, corporate trainers and/or Affinity Ministers.

For more information about teacher training, visit our website at www.heartwayspress.com or call us at 1-888-HART-WAY.

Paul Ferrini is the author of over 30 books on love, healing and forgiveness. His unique blend of radical Christianity and other wisdom traditions goes beyond self-help and recovery into the heart of healing. His conferences, retreats, and *Affinity Group Process* have helped thousands of people deepen their practice of forgiveness and open their hearts to the divine presence in themselves and others.

For more information on Paul's work, visit the web-site at *www.paulferrini.com,* email: info@heartwayspress.com or write to **Heartways Press, 9 Phillips Steet, Greenfield, MA 01301.**

New Releases from Heartways Press

Paul Ferrini's *Course in Spiritual Mastery*

Part One: The Laws of Love
A Guide to Living in Harmony
with Universal Spiritual Truth
160 pages $12.95
ISBN # 1-879159-60-0

Drawing from many Wisdom Traditions, this book integrates the insights of Paul Ferrini's 30 books on Spirituality into a comprehensive and powerful whole. Like a beautiful and intricately woven tapestry, the ten major spiritual principles are described and illustrated. Paul's unique ability to synthesize the wisdom of the Taoist, Zen, Sufi and Hasidic Masters with the heart centered teachings of Jesus makes this material a delight to encounter. Presented with absolute clarity, this material will help you align your life with the highest teachings available on the planet!

Part Two: The Power of Love
10 Spiritual Practices that can
Transform Your Life
168 pages $12.95
ISBN # 1-879159-61-9

The Power of Love presents 10 Spiritual Practices that can transform your life. Performed over a 10 week period, these experiential exercises will help you to integrate into daily life the concepts presented in *The Laws of Love*. This book is required reading for all candidates for teacher certification.

The Complete *Laws of Love* Course
Taught by Paul Ferrini

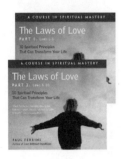

THE LAWS OF LOVE:
A Course in Spiritual Mastery
Part One (5 CDs) ISBN # 1-879159-58-9
$49.95
Part Two (4 CDs) ISBN # 1-879159-59-7
$39.95

The audio version of *The Laws of Love* presents the complete in-depth course on 9 CDs.
This version contains a great deal of material that is not included in
The Laws of Love book. It also explores additional content based on
participants' questions. You will experience the power and intimacy of
this weekend workshop presented by Paul Ferrini. Serious students of
Paul's *Course in Spritual Mastery* will want to own this CD series.

Other Recent Titles by Paul Ferrini
Available from Heartways Press

Wisdom Cards: Spiritual Guidance
for Every Day of our Lives
ISBN 1-879159-50-3 $10.95
*Each full color card features a beautiful
painting evoking an archetypal theme.*

Wisdom Cards will help you open to the
source of wisdom within your own consciousness and determine propitious times for a
significant event or project. These cards can be used alone (instruction
booklet included) or in conjunction with the book *Everyday Wisdom.*

Everyday Wisdom
A Spiritual Book of Days
by Paul Ferrini
224 pages paperback $13.95
ISBN 1-879159-51-1

Every Day Brings a Lesson!

Every day offers us incredible wisdom if only we can see the spiritual principles working behind the events and circumstances that are playing out in our lives. Seeing those principles requires a daily practice that helps us look beneath the surface of our lives and encourages us to face the truth, even when it is difficult.

Everyday Wisdom is a tool that can help you understand your spiritual lessons as they unfold each day of your life. Used in conjunction with journaling, it gives you a simple method of introspection, of looking within your own heart and mind, and finding the wisdom and the guidance that abide there. **This book can be used as a Spiritual Oracle** in conjunction with *Wisdom Cards,* the companion card deck.

Forbidden Fruit: Unraveling the Mysteries of Sin, Guilt and Atonement
by Paul Ferrini
ISBN 1-879159-48-1
160 pages paperback $12.95

Adam and Eve were not just naughty, disobedient children. They were created in God's image. They had God's desire for creative expression and awareness. As long as they remained in the Garden, they could not take the next step in their evolution.

Adam and Eve began a spiritual journey that would take them from sin to atonement, from ignorance to knowledge, from denial to responsibility. They would have to explore their darkness to find the light. They would have to become sinners to discover the blueprint for their redemption. They would have to experience the limits of their bodies, their minds and the three dimensional world to know that their true nature transcended all this. To become God, they had to first become human.

The Living Christ: Conversations with a Teacher of Love
by Paul Ferrini
ISBN 1-879159-49-X
256 pages paperback $14.95

Paul: Is it true that you are the Christ?

Jesus: Yes, and so are you and everyone else who learns to love and accept self and others. If you practice what I came to teach, you will begin to realize that the Christ nature is the essence of each person . . . Christ is the light born in the darkness. It is the flame of self acceptance that extends to others and eventually to all. He is rebirth of love in a world driven by fear.

Dancing with the Beloved: Opening our Hearts to the Lessons of Love
by Paul Ferrini
ISBN 1-879159-47-3
160 pages paperback $12.95

Romance may open the door to love, but it does not help us walk through it. Something else is needed. Something deeper. Something ultimately more real. . . . Challenging times must be weathered. Love must be strengthened beyond neediness and self-interest. It must die a thousand deaths to learn to rise like the phoenix beyond adversity of any kind.

Love is not a fragile, shiny thing, kept separate from the pain and misery of life. It is born of our willingness to learn from our mistakes and encounter the depth of our pain, as well as our partner's pain.

Enlightenment for Everyone
by Paul Ferrini
with an Introduction by Iyanla Vanzant
ISBN 1-879159-45-7
160 pages hardcover $16.00

Enlightenment is not contingent on finding the right teacher or having some kind of peak spiritual experience. There's nothing that you need to get, find or acquire to be enlightened. You don't need a priest or rabbi to intercede with God for you. You don't need to memorize scripture or engage in esoteric breathing practices. You simply need to discover who you already are and be it fully. This essential guide to self-realization contains eighteen spiritual practices that will enable you to awaken to the truth of your being.

The Great Way of All Beings:
Renderings of Lao Tzu
by Paul Ferrini
ISBN 1-879159-46-5
320 pages hardcover $23.00

Paul Ferrini's luminous new translation captures the essence of Lao Tzu and the fundamental aspects of Taoism in a way that no single book ever has! Part one, *River of Light,* is an intuitive, spontaneous rendering of the material that captures the spirit of the *Tao Te Ching,* Part Two is a more conservative translation of the *Tao Te Ching* that attempts as much as possible to stay with the words and images used in the original text.

Reflections of the Christ Mind Series

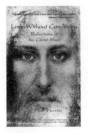   

Part 1   Part 2   Part 3   Part 4

The four books in the *Christ Mind* series have changed the lives of hundreds of thousands of readers, bringing both believers and unbelievers alike face to face with the greatest teacher of our time. Here at last is a gospel devoted solely to Jesus' teachings of love, healing, and forgiveness. The teacher we meet in these pages is both compassionate and open-minded—he is the Jesus we know in our hearts. Repudiating religious hypocrisy, intolerance, and spiritual pride, he rejects the dogmatic position of the Church, offering instead words of hope and healing that form the new gospel for today.

Part One: Love Without Conditions
200 pages ISBN 1-879159-15-5 $12.00

Part Two: The Silence of the Heart
286 pages ISBN 1-879159-16-3 $14.95

Part Three: Miracle of Love
200 pages ISBN 1-879159-23-6 $12.95

Part Four: Return to the Garden
200 pages ISBN 1-879159-35-x $12.95

Selections from the Christ Mind Material

I am the Door

In this lovely lyrical collection, we hear the voice of Jesus speaking directly to us about practical topics of everyday life like work and livelihood, relationships, community, forgiveness, spiritual practices, and miracles. A beautiful introduction to the Christ Mind teachings.

288 pages Hardcover   ISBN 1-879159-41-4
$21.95

The Way of Peace
A New System of Spiritual Guidance

Drawing from the *Christ Mind* teachings, *The Way of Peace* empowers you to connect with peace within and act in harmony with your true self and the unique circumstances of your life. Like the *I-Ching* and *The Book of Runes*, this book is designed to be used as an oracle. It can be ordered with special dice blessed by the author,

256 pages Hardcover   ISBN 1-879159-42-2
$19.95

Reflections of the Christ Mind:
The Present Day Teachings of Jesus
Introduction by Neale Donald Walsch

A comprehensive selection representing the most important teachings in the *Christ Mind* series, published by Doubleday.

302 pages Hardcover ISBN 0-385-49952-3
$19.95

Two Best-selling
Relationship Books

The relationship book you've been waiting for

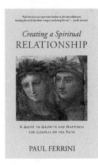

Creating a Spiritual Relationship

This simple but profound guide to growth and happiness for couples will help you and your partner weather the ups and downs of your relationship so that you can grow together and deepen the intimacy between you.

128 pages Paperback
ISBN 1-879159-39-2 $10.95

A practical manual for moving from fear to love

The Twelve Steps of Forgiveness

This book gives us a step-by-step process for moving through our fears, projections, judgments, and guilt so that we can take responsibility for creating the life we want. With great gentleness, we learn to embrace our lessons and to find equality with others.

144 pages Paperback ISBN 1-879159-10-4
$10.00

Two Practical Manuals
for Transforming Self and Society

Living in the Heart:
The Affinity Process and the
Path of Unconditional Love and
Acceptance

The definitive book on the Affinity Process! Now, you can learn how to hold a safe, loving, non-judgmental space for yourself and others which will enable you to open your heart and move through your fears.

If you are a serious student of the Christ Mind teachings, this book is essential for you. It will enable you to begin a spiritual practice which will transform your life and the lives of others. It will also offer you a way of extending the teachings of love and forgiveness through-out your community.

128 pages Paperback ISBN 1-879159-36-8 $10.95

Taking Back Our Schools

Based on Paul's experience home-schooling his daughter, this book is written for parents who are concerned about the education of their children. It presents a simple idea that could completely transform the educational system in this country.

128 pages Paperback ISBN 1-879159-43-0
$10.95

Wisdom Books

Illuminations on the Road to Nowhere

There comes a time for all of us when the outer destinations no longer satisfy and we finally understand that the love and happiness we seek cannot be found outside of us. It must be found in our own hearts, on the other side of our pain.

This provocative book challenges many of our basic assumptions about personal happiness and the meaning of our relationship with others and with God.

160 pages   Paperback   ISBN 1-879159-44-9 $12.95

Grace Unfolding: The Art of Living A Surrendered Life

This book is not about surrender to an outside authority, but to an inside one. It is about the relinquishment of our ego consciousness, our separated states of heart and mind to a greater consciousness, to the essence of love which is the source of who we are.

96 pages   Paperback   ISBN 1-879159-37-6 $9.95

The Ecstatic Moment: A Practical Manual for Opening Your Heart and Staying in It.

A simple guide that helps us take appropriate responsibility for our experience and establish healthy boundaries with others. It contains many helpful exercises and meditations that teach us to stay centered, clear and open in heart and mind.

128 pages   Paperback   ISBN 1-879159-18-X $10.95

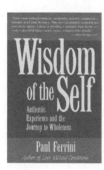

The Wisdom of the Self

Explores our authentic experience and our journey to wholeness. "The Self is not a bundle of actions or conditions, but an unconditional state of being. To know the Self is to allow everything, to embrace the totality of who we are, all that we think and feel, all of our fear, all of our love."

229 pages   Paperback   ISBN 1-879159-14-7
$12.00

The Body of Truth

A crystal clear introduction to the universal teachings of love and forgiveness. This book traces all forms of suffering to negative attitudes and false beliefs, which we have the ability to transform.

64 pages   Paperback
ISBN 1-879159-02-3 $7.50

Forgiveness & Inner Child Books

The Wounded Child's Journey:
Into Love's Embrace

This book explores a healing process in which we confront our deep-seated guilt and fear, bringing love and forgiveness to the wounded child within. By surrendering our judgments of self and others, we overcome feelings of separation and dismantle co-dependent patterns that restrict our self-expression and ability to give and receive love.

225 pages Paperback SBN 1-879159-06-6 $12.00

The Bridge to Reality

A Heart-Centered Approach to *A Course in Miracles* and the process of inner healing. Sharing his experiences of spiritual awakening, Paul emphasizes self-acceptance and forgiveness as cornerstones of spiritual practice. Presented with beautiful photos, this book conveys the essence of *The Course* as it is lived in daily life.

192 pages Paperback ISBN 1-879159-03-1 $12.00

From Ego to Self

108 illustrated aphorisms designed to offer you a new way of viewing conflict situations so that you can overcome negative thinking and bring more energy, faith and optimism into your life.

144 pages Paperback ISBN 1-879159-01-5 $10.00

Audio Books and Workshops

Audio Workshops on CD

"The veils are lifting. The time for denial is over."

Atonement: The Awakening of Planet Earth and its Inhabitants
A 2003 talk with questions and answers

ISBN 1-879159-53-8 $16.95

"The collective shadow is rising, but behind it is the light!"

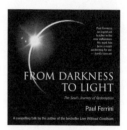

From Darkness to Light: The Soul's Journey of Redemption
A 2003 talk with questions and answers

ISBN 1-879159-54-6 $16.95

"Love is a state of being. It is the essence of who we are."

Love is That Certainty
A popular Christ Mind talk with questions and answers

ISBN 1-879159-52-X $16.95

Talks and Workshops on Tape

Single Cassettes

Answering Our Own Call for Love
1 Cassette $10.00 ISBN 1-879159-33-4

The Ecstatic Moment
1 Cassette $10.00 ISBN 1-879159-27-3

Honoring Self and Other
1 Cassette $10.00 ISBN 1-879159-34-1

Seek First the Kingdom
1 Cassette $10.00 ISBN 1-879159-30-3

Double Cassette Tape Sets

Ending the Betrayal of the Self
2 Cassettes $16.95 ISBN 1-879159-28-7

Relationships: Changing Past Patterns
2 Cassettes $16.95 ISBN 1-879159-32-5

Relationship As a Spiritual Path
2 Cassettes $16.95 ISBN 1-879159-29-5

The Economy of Love: Creativity, Right Livelihood & Abundance

Readings from *Silence of the Heart, The Ecstatic Moment, Grace Unfolding* and other books

ISBN 1-879159-56-2 $16.95

Relationship as a Spiritual Path

Readings from *Creating a Spiritual Relationship, Dancing with the Beloved, Miracle of Love* and other books

ISBN 1-879159-55-4 $16.95

The Hands of God: The Emergence of Spirit in the World

Readings from *Illuminations, Enlightenment for Everyone, Forbidden Fruit, The Great Way of All Beings* and other books

ISBN 1-879159-57-0 $16.95

Books on Tape

Finally our Bestselling Title on Audio Tape read by the author

Love Without Conditions, Reflections of the Christ Mind, Part I

The incredible book from Jesus calling us to awaken to our own Christhood. Approximately 3.25 hours

2 Cassettes ISBN 1-879159-24-4 $19.95

Poetry Books and Tapes

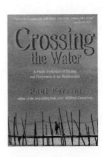

Crossing The Water: Poems About Healing and Forgiveness in Our Relationships

Our relationships help us heal childhood wounds, walk through our deepest fears, and cross over the water of our emotional pain. Just as the rocks in the river are "pounded and caressed to rounded stone," the rough edges of our personalities are worn smooth in the context of a committed relationship. If we can keep our hearts open, we can heal together and discover what it means to give and receive love without conditions.

96 pages Paperback ISBN 1-879159-25-2 $9.95

Available Light

Inspirational, passionate poems dealing with the work of inner integration, love and relationships, death and re-birth, loss and abundance, life purpose and the reality of spiritual vision.

128 pages   Paperback   ISBN 1-879159-05-8
$10.00

The Poetry of the Soul

Many people consider this cassette tape to be the most compelling of all of Paul Ferrini's work. These luminous poems read by the author are filled with wonderful nuances and insights. Come to this feast of the beloved with an open heart and open ears.

One cassette tape   ISBN 1-879159-26-0
$10.00

Virtues of The Way

A lyrical work of contemporary scripture reminiscent of the *Tao Te Ching*. Beautifully illustrated, this inspirational book will help you cultivate the spiritual values required to fulfill your creative purpose and live in harmony with others.

64 pages   Paperback   ISBN 1-879159-04-X
$7.50

Meditation/Healing Tapes

The Circle of Healing

This gentle guided meditation opens the heart to love's presence in your experience. ISBN 1-879159-08-2 $10.00

Healing the Wounded Child

A potent healing tape that helps transform old feelings of pain, fragmentation, self-judgment and separation. ISBN 1-879159-11-2 $10.00

Forgiveness: Returning to the Original Blessing

By letting go of our judgments and ending our ego-based search for perfection, we can bring our darkness to the light, dissolving anger, guilt, and shame. ISBN 1-879159-12-0 $10.00

Posters and Notecards

Risen Christ Posters & Notecards

11" x 17" Poster suitable for framing
ISBN 1-879159-19-8 $10.00

Set of 8 Notecards with Envelopes
ISBN 1-879159-20-1 $10.00

Ecstatic Moment Posters & Notecards

8.5" x 11" Poster suitable for framing
ISBN 1-879159-21-X $5.00

Set of 8 Notecards with Envelopes
ISBN 1-879159-22-8 $10.00

Heartways Press Order Form

You can also order by credit card on our website:
www.paulferrini.com *or* heartwayspress.com

Name _____

Address _____

City _____ State _____ Zip _____

Phone/Fax_____Email _____

Books by Paul Ferrini

The Laws of Love ($12.95)   _____

The Power of Love ($12.95)   _____

Everyday Wisdom ($13.95)   _____

Wisdom Cards ($10.95)   _____

Forbidden Fruit ($12.95)   _____

The Living Christ ($14.95)   _____

Dancing with the Beloved ($12.95)   _____

The Great Way of All Beings: Hardcover ($23.00)   _____

Enlightenment for Everyone Hardcover ($16.00)   _____

Taking Back Our Schools ($10.95)   _____

The Way of Peace Hardcover ($19.95)   _____

    Way of Peace Dice ($4.00)   _____

Illuminations on the Road to Nowhere ($12.95)   _____

I am the Door Hardcover ($21.95)   _____

Reflections of the Christ Mind Hardcover ($19.95)   _____

Creating a Spiritual Relationship ($10.95)   _____

Grace Unfolding: Living a Surrendered Life ($9.95)   _____

Return to the Garden ($12.95)   _____

Living in the Heart ($10.95)   _____

Miracle of Love ($12.95)   _____

Crossing the Water ($9.95)   _____

The Ecstatic Moment ($10.95)   _____

The Silence of the Heart ($14.95)   _____

Love Without Conditions ($12.00)   _____

The Wisdom of the Self ($12.00)   _____

The Twelve Steps of Forgiveness ($10.00)   _____

The Circle of Atonement ($12.00)   _____

The Bridge to Reality ($12.00)   _____

From Ego to Self ($10.00)   _____

Virtues of the Way ($7.50)   _____

The Body of Truth ($7.50)   _____

Available Light ($10.00)   _____

Audio Books and Workshops by Paul Ferrini

The Laws of Love Part 1 ($49.95) 5 CDs _____

The Laws of Love Part 2 ($39.95) 4 CDs _____

Atonement:The Awakening of Planet Earth ($16.95) CD _____

From Darkness to Light ($16.95) CD _____

Love is That Certainty ($16.95) CD _____

The Economy of Love ($16.95) CD _____

Relationship as a Spiritual Path ($16.95) CD _____

The Hands of God ($16.95) CD _____

The Circle of Healing ($10.00) Tape _____

Healing the Wounded Child ($10.00) Tape _____

Forgiveness: The Original Blessing ($10.00) Tape _____

The Poetry of the Soul ($10.00) Tape _____

Seek First the Kingdom ($10.00) Tape _____

Answering Our Own Call for Love ($10.00) Tape _____

The Ecstatic Moment ($10.00) Tape _____

Honoring Self and Other ($10.00) Tape _____

Love Without Conditions ($19.95) 2 tapes _____

Ending the Betrayal of the Self ($16.95) 2 tapes _____

Relationships: Changing Past Patterns ($16.95) 2 tapes _____

Relationship As a Spiritual Path ($16.95) 2 tapes _____

Posters and Notecards

Risen Christ Poster 11"x17" ($10.00) _____

Ecstatic Moment Poster 8.5"x11" ($5.00) _____

Risen Christ Notecards 8/pkg ($10.00) _____

Ecstatic Moment Notecards 8/pkg ($10.00) _____

Shipping

Priority Mail shipping for one item $3.95. _____

Add $1.00 for each additional item _____

Add $1.00 for each hardcover book _____

Massachusetts residents please add 5% sales tax. _____

Add an extra $2.00 for shipping to Canada/Mexico _____

Add an extra $4.00 for shipping to Europe _____

Add an extra $6.00 for shipping to other countries _____

TOTAL _____

Send Order To: Heartways Press, 9 Phillips St., Greenfield, MA 01301

413-774-9474   Toll free: 1-888-HARTWAY (Orders only)

www.heartwayspress.com   email: info@heartwayspress.com